The Tiny Book of Football Jokes

The Tiny Book of Football Jokes

Edward Phillips

Illustrated by
Graham Morris

HarperCollins*Publishers*

HarperCollins*Publishers*
77–85 Fulham Palace Road,
Hammersmith, London W6 8JB

www.**fire**and**water**.com

This paperback edition 2000
1 3 5 7 9 8 6 4 2

Previously published in Great Britain
by Fontana 1991

ISBN 0 00 710497 9

Set in Stone Sans by Rowland Phototypesetting Ltd,
Bury St Edmunds, Suffolk
Printed and bound in Great Britain by Scotprint

What is football? It has been described as a game with twenty-two players, two linesmen and 20,000 referees.

'How was the match, dear?' asked the wife of a football fan who had just returned home.

'The other side won,' he grumbled. 'By seven very lucky goals!'

A desperate manager, whose team had lost fourteen consecutive games, rang a colleague for advice on training methods.

'I'll tell you what you should do,' said his friend. 'Take the team out on a six-mile run every day.'

'What's the point of that?' asked the manager.

'Today's Monday,' was the reply. 'By Saturday, they'll be thirty-six miles away and you can forget all about them!'

It is said that in Ireland, if it looks like rain before a match, they play the extra time first.

'What did you think of my game today, coach?'
'Not bad – but I still prefer football.'

The following instruction recently appeared on the noticeboard of a large car factory in Cowley:

ALL APPLICATIONS FOR LEAVE OF ABSENCE FOR FAMILY BEREAVEMENTS, SICKNESS, JURY DUTY, ETC., MUST BE HANDED IN TO THE PERSONNEL MANAGER NO LATER THAN 6 P.M. ON THE DAY PRECEDING THE MATCH.

A goalkeeper had had a particularly bad season and announced that he was retiring from professional football. In a television interview he was asked his reasons for quitting the game. 'Well, basically,' he said, 'it's a question of illness and fatigue.'

'Can you be more specific?' asked the interviewer.

'Well,' said the player, 'specifically, the fans are sick and tired of me.'

A match between two non-League teams took place last winter in the north of England. It had been raining heavily all week and the ground resembled a swamp. However, the referee ruled that play was possible and tossed the coin to determine ends. The visiting captain won the toss, and after a moment's thought, said, 'OK – we'll take the shallow end!'

Referees at Celtic Rangers matches always have a particularly hard time. One poor unfortunate, officiating at his first fixture, was checking in with the team managers before the kick-off. 'Well, that seems to be about everything,' said the Rangers boss. 'Now, if you'd just like to give us the name and address of your next-of-kin, we can start the match.'

Paddy: 'I couldn't get to the match last Saturday. What was the score?'

Mick: 'Nil–nil.'

Paddy: 'What was it at half-time?'

Did you hear about the England international player who had a date with a referee's daughter? She penalised him three times – for handling, interference and trying to pull off a jersey.

The match was over and the team captain, who had muffed three easy goal shots, came over to the manager and said, 'You'll have to excuse me if I dash off, chief. I've got a plane to catch and I don't want to miss it.'

'Off you go, then,' said the manager. 'And better luck with the plane.'

A player was being ticked off by the coach for missing a very easy goal-kick. 'All right,' said the player, 'how *should* I have played the shot?'

'Under an assumed name,' snapped the coach.

The football club dance was in full swing when three strangers arrived and demanded admission. 'May I see your tickets, please?' said the club secretary at the door.

'We haven't got any tickets,' said one of the men. 'We're friends of the referee.'

'Get out of here!' said the club secretary. 'Whoever heard of a referee with three friends!'

One of the lesser-known stories in Greek mythology tells of a classic football match on Mount Olympus between the Gods and the Mortals. The Gods trounced the Mortals 8–0 and attributed their victory to the brilliance of their new centaur-forward.

Wife: 'Football, football, football! That's all
            you ever think about! If you said you
            were going to stay at home one
            Saturday afternoon to help with the
            housework, I think I'd drop dead from
            the shock!'

Husband: 'It's no good trying to bribe me, dear.'

Reporter: 'Tell me, Mr Harris, will your £100,000 win on the football pools make any difference to your way of life?'

Pools winner: 'None at all. I shall carry on exactly as before.'

Reporter: 'But what about all the begging letters?'

Pools winner: 'Oh, I'll keep sending them out as usual.'

In a crucial Cup semi-final a few years ago, the capacity crowd of 30,000 watched a rather diminutive striker get possession of the ball early in the second half. He was immediately tackled by three large defenders, and went down under a pile of thrashing arms and legs. Emerging dazed from the mêlée a few moments later, he looked round at the crowded stands and gasped, 'How did they all get back in their seats so quickly?'

A famous international footballer was asked to appear nude in the centrefold of a glossy new women's magazine. 'Our intention is to photograph you standing nude holding a ball,' said the features editor.

'I see,' said the footballer. 'What will I be doing with my other hand?'

The angry captain snarled at the referee. 'What would happen if I called you a blind bastard who couldn't make a correct decision to save his life?'

'It would be a red card for you.'

'And if I didn't say it but only thought it?'

'That's different. If you only thought it but didn't say it, I couldn't do a thing.'

'Well, we'll leave it like that, then, shall we?' smiled the captain.

Two Irish team managers promised their players a pint of Guinness for every goal they scored during an important match. The final score was 119–98.

Striker: 'I've just had a good idea for
        strengthening the team.'
Manager: 'Good! When are you leaving?'

'I just don't understand it,' an Irish footballer
complained. 'One match I play very well, then the
next match I'm terrible.'

    'Well,' said his wife, 'why don't you just play
every other match?'

The manager and coach of an Irish team were discussing the players they had on their books and the manager asked, 'How many goals has O'Halloran scored this season?'

'Exactly double what he scored last season,' replied the coach. 'Eleven.'

Three football codes prevail in Ireland: Rugby, which is defined as a thugs' game played by gentlemen; soccer – a gentleman's game played by thugs; and Gaelic football – a thugs' game played by thugs!

A supporter arrived at the ground one Saturday to find the place empty. He went to the office and asked, 'What time does the match start?'

'There's no match today,' replied the official.

'But there must be!' argued the fan.

'I'm telling you there's no match today,' repeated the official.

'But there's always a match on Saturday afternoon,' said the fan, 'even if it's only a reserves.'

'Watch my lips,' shouted the irate official. 'There is no M-A-T-F-C-H today!'

'Well, for your information,' the would-be spectator shouted back, 'there's no F in match.'

'That's what I've been trying to tell you!' yelled the official.

Two old men were holding up the queue outside the turnstyle before the game, while one of them hunted for his ticket. He looked in his coat pockets and his waistcoat pockets and his trouser pockets, all to no avail. 'Hang on a minute,' said the gateman. 'What's that in your mouth?' It was the missing ticket!

As they moved inside his mate said, 'Crikey, Cyril! You must be getting senile in your old age. Fancy having your ticket in your mouth and forgetting about it!'

'I'm not *that* stupid,' said old Cyril. 'I was chewing last week's date off it.'

'My wife told me last week that she'd leave me if I didn't stop spending so much time at football matches.'

'What a shame!'

'Yes. I shall miss her.'

In church one Sunday the vicar opened his Bible to read the lesson. In a loud voice he proclaimed, 'Corinthians 7!'

A keen football fan who was dozing in the front row woke up with a start and shouted, 'Who were they playing?'

'We're starting up an amateur football team. Would you like to join?'

'I would, yes, but I'm afraid I don't know the first thing about football.'

'That's all right. We need a referee as well.'

The manager of an Irish club was talking to a young player who had applied for a trial with the club. 'Do you kick with both feet?' asked the manager.

'Don't be silly!' said the trialist. 'If I did that, I wouldn't be able to stand up, would I?'

As the defender ran in to tackle he took a full-blooded kick between the legs and fell unconscious to the ground. When he regained consciousness he was in hospital. He beckoned to the doctor and croaked, 'Is it bad?'

'I'm afraid so,' said the doctor.

'Are my playing days over?' asked the anxious footballer.

'Not necessarily,' answered the medic.

'So will I be able to play football for my club again?'

'Oh yes,' said the doctor, 'providing your club has a ladies team.'

'Just a minute, ref!' yelled the goalkeeper. 'That wasn't a goal!'

'Oh, wasn't it?' shouted the referee. 'You just watch the "Sports Report" on television tonight!'

'Your team's rubbish! We beat you 9–2 last Saturday, even though we had a man short!'

'What do you mean "a man short"? You had ten players and the referee, didn't you?'

A football hooligan appeared in court charged with disorderly conduct and assault. The arresting officer, giving evidence, stated that the accused had thrown something into the canal. 'What exactly was it that he threw into the canal?' asked the magistrate.

'Stones, sir.'

'Well, that's hardly an offence is it?'

'It was in this case, sir,' said the police officer. 'Stones was the referee.'

A famous soccer international was talking to another guest at a party. 'I've been persuaded to write my autobiography,' he said, 'but I don't want it published until after I'm dead.'

'Really?' said the guest. 'I shall look forward to reading it.'

'You're all feet!' yelled the coach at the practice session. 'All bloody feet! How many times have I told you – use your brains, use your feet, but let the ball do the work!'

'Well, don't tell me,' shouted the unfortunate player. 'Tell the bloody ball!'

'Is your goalkeeper getting any better?'

'Not really. Last Saturday he let in five goals in the first ten minutes. He was so fed up when he failed to stop the fifth that he put his head in his hands – and dropped it!'

At a recent Irish League match between Newry and Larne, the visitors were awarded a penalty and the captain summoned his best player and said, 'I want you to take this one, Patrick. Just think hard as you kick – think which way the wind is blowing, and think which direction the keeper's going to jump.'

'Holy Mother!' said Patrick. 'Do you expect me to think and kick at the same time?'

Graffiti

Outside the County Ground at Swindon:

SWINDON TOWN ARE MAGIC!

And underneath:

WATCH THEM DISAPPEAR FROM THE SECOND DIVISION!

On the wall of a chapel in Dumbarton, Scotland:

JESUS SAVES!

And underneath:

DUMBARTON SHOULD SIGN HIM FOR GOAL!

The office-boy had taken the afternoon off to attend his uncle's funeral. His boss, a keen football fan, went the same afternoon to watch a match between Aberdeen and Celtic, and he saw the office-boy among the crowd. 'So this is your uncle's funeral, is it?' he said sarcastically.

'I shouldn't be at all surprised,' said the office-boy. 'He's the referee.'

A spectator at a match in the north of England kept up a constant barrage of insults and derogatory remarks directed against the referee. Finally the ref could stand it no longer. He marched over to the stand and, looking the noisy spectator squarely in the eye, shouted, 'Look here – I've been watching you for the last twenty minutes . . .'

'I thought so,' the spectator shouted back. 'I knew you couldn't have been watching the game!'

There was once a fanatical Spurs supporter who thought of nothing but football all day long. He talked about football, read about football, watched nothing but football on television and attended matches as often as he possibly could. at last his poor wife could stand it no longer. One night she said, 'I honestly believe you love Spurs more than you love me!'

'Blimey,' said the fan, 'I love Hartlepool United more than I love you!'

It was only the fourth week of the season and United's new goalkeeper had already let in twenty-seven goals. He was having a drink in a pub one night when a man approached him and said, 'I've been watching you play, son, and I think I might be able to help you.'

'Are you a trainer?' said the young goalkeeper hopefully.

'No,' said the stranger, 'I'm an optician.'

Referee: 'Penalty!'
Home captain: 'Who for?'
Referee: 'Us!'

'I've been playing football professionally for ten years now. Of course, my father was dead set against my taking up the game at all. In fact he offered me £5,000 not to train.'

'Really? What did you do with the money?'

The manager of a Fourth Division club called his leading goal-scorer into his office. 'You've played so well this season,' he said, 'that the committee has decided to give you a special bonus. We would like you to accept this cheque for £5000.'

'Thank you very much,' said the player. 'That's very kind of you.'

'And,' continued the manager, 'if you play as well for the rest of the season, the chairman will sign it for you.'

A famous English footballer had just been transferred for a record sum of money and was being interviewed on television. 'Do you realise,' said the interviewer, 'that the money you will receive as a result of this transfer, together with your income from endorsements, personal appearances, lecturing and so on will mean that you'll have earned more in one year than the Queen gets from the Civil List?'

'Well, I should hope so!' said the footballer. 'I play a damn sight better than she does.'

There was once a match in Liverpool between Anglican vicars and Roman Catholic priests. Early in the game the Catholics were awarded a penalty. Father Flanagan placed the ball carefully, took a long run at it, and kicked. The ball sailed high into the air and missed the goal by miles. Father Flanagan didn't utter a word. He just stood there with a grim expression on his face. The team captain, Monsignor Ryan, came up behind him and said reprovingly, 'Father, that is the most profane silence I have ever heard!'

It was the last game of the season. Mathieson had been with the team from the start but he was such a slow player that never once had he actually been allowed to play, but had spent all his time on the substitute bench. At this last match, however, there were so many fouls and injuries that every substitute but him had been sent on. With ten minutes to go, yet another player was carried off the field and the coach looked at the substitute bench, his eye finally alighting on Mathieson. Mathieson's face lit up. 'Are you going to send me on, coach?' he asked eagerly.

'No!' snapped the coach. 'Just get out of the way. 'I'm going to send in the bench!'

A man walked into the office of a large London firm and said to the manager, 'I'm young Cartwright's grandfather – he works in your mail room here. I just popped in to ask if you could give him the afternoon off so I could take him to the League Final at Wembley.

'I'm afraid he's not here,' said the manager. 'We already gave him the afternoon off to go to your funeral.'

A week before the Cup Final at Wembley a few years ago there was an advertisement in *The Times* which read: 'Man offers marriage to woman supplying Cup Final ticket for next Saturday. Replies must enclose photograph of ticket.'

'You're looking worried.

'Yes. My doctor's just told me I can't play football.'

'Oh! he's seen you play, has he?'

A small boy got lost at a football match. He went up to a policeman and said, 'I've lost my dad!'

The policeman said, 'What's he like?'

To which the little boy replied, 'Beer and women!'

There was trouble on the terraces at The Hawthorns one Saturday afternoon. A huge West Bromwich Albion fan picked up a tiny spectator wearing the blue and white colours of Millwall, the visiting team. As he was about to hurl him to the ground, one of his mates yelled, 'Hey, Derek, don't waste him! Chuck him at the referee!'

After considerable effort and expense a First Division manager succeeded in obtaining the services of Miodrag Krivokapic and Mixu Paatelainen of Dundee, Dariusz Wdowczwk of Celtic, Detzi Kruszynski of Wimbledon, and Steve Ogrizovic of Coventry. 'Are these boys any good?' asked a colleague.

'I couldn't care less,' said the manager. 'I just want to get my own back on some of these smart-aleck TV sports commentators!'

A woman was reading a newspaper one morning and said to her husband, 'Look at this, dear. There's an article here about a man who traded his wife for a season ticket to Arsenal. You wouldn't do a thing like that, would you?'

'Of course I wouldn't!' replied her husband. 'The season's almost over!'

The shrill blast of the whistle and the pointing finger of the referee stopped the player in his tracks. The referee beckoned him over and produced notebook, pencil and yellow card. 'It's a yellow card for you,' said the referee, waving the card at the footballer.

'You know what you can do with your yellow card!' shouted the player.

'You're too late, mate,' replied the referee. 'There's three red cards there already!'

The boss called the office-boy into his private sanctum. 'How did your great-aunt's funeral go yesterday afternoon?' he asked.

'It went off all right, sir,' said the office-boy, puzzled.

'Good, good,' said the boss. 'Pity they've got to do it all over again.'

'Pardon, sir?' said the office-boy.

'Yes. I understand there's a replay on Saturday.'

There was once a big football match between Heaven and Hell for the Celestial Cup. An angel was talking to a devil on the night before the match and remarked, 'It should be a walkover for us, you know. We've got all the good footballers up here.'

'Yes, I know,' said the devil with a fiendish grin. 'But we've got all the referees down there!'

A man holding a football leaned over his garden gate and shouted to two boys standing on the other side of the street, 'Is this your ball?'

'Did it do any damage, mister?' asked one of the lads.

'No, it didn't.'

'Then it's ours,' said the boy.

All through the match, a well-dressed man in the crowd kept up a constant barrage of criticism directed at the referee. When the game was over the referee went over to the heckler and asked him if he had a business card.

'Certainly,' said the man, somewhat surprised, and handed over a card on which was printed HENRY ADAMS, SOLICITOR.

'Thanks,' said the referee. 'I'll be in to see you on Monday morning.'

'All right,' said the solicitor. 'Legal problem, is it?'

'Oh, no nothing like that,' said the referee. 'I'm just coming round to tell you how to run *your* business!'

Two boys were playing football in the back garden with a new football.

'Where did you get that ball?' asked their mother.

'We found it.'

'Are you sure it was lost?'

'Oh, yes. We saw them looking for it.'

There was once a famous football star who rather fancied himself as God's gift to the ladies. He fell in love with a local girl and approached her father to ask for permission to marry her.

'My daughter marry a footballer player?' shouted the father. 'Over my dead body!'

'But, sir, you haven't even seen me play!' protested the star.

'Well, all right, then – I'll come to the match on Saturday.'

After the match the father came into the dressing rooms and shook the footballer warmly by the hand. 'Of course you can marry my daughter, my boy! You're no more a footballer player than I am!'

There was once a football match between two small village teams. The visitors were surprised to see that the home team's goalkeeper was a horse. The horse played extremely well and it was mainly due to him that the home team won. After the match the visiting captain said to the home captain, 'How on earth did a horse ever learn to keep goal like that?'

'How does anyone learn?' answered the home captain. 'Practice, practice, practice!'

After the season was over a couple of players used their savings to go on safari in Africa. The highlight of their trip was seeing a lion in his natural habitat after making a kill. Suddenly the lion began to walk purposefully towards them. One of the players immediately began to put on a pair of jogging shoes. His friend said, 'You're wasting your time! You'll never outrun that lion!'

'Maybe not,' said his friend, 'but if I can outrun you, I'll be laughing!'

It was a needle match between Celtic and Rangers at Glasgow's Ibrox Park. A mild little man was accosted by a huge and aggressive supporter in full regalia. 'Are ye a Celtic fan or a Rangers fan?' he growled menacingly.

'Neither, really,' said the little man nervously. 'I just like watching football.'

'Och,' snarled the Scot, 'a bloody atheist, eh?'

Joe was admiring a silver cup in a display cabinet. It was inscribed 'TO THE FOOTBALLER OF THE YEAR'. 'Hey, Mickey,' he said, 'I didn't know you were interested in football.'

'I'm not,' said Mickey.

'But you've got a silver cup inscribed to the footballer of the year in your cabinet.'

'Oh, I got that for running.'

'Running?' said Joe. 'How the hell did you get a football cup for running?'

'Simple,' said Mickey. 'When no one was looking, I grabbed it and ran.'

A certain Fourth Division club was right at the bottom of the ladder so the coach instituted a course of retraining for the coming season. As many of the team members seemed to be ignorant of the basics of the game, he decided to start at the beginning. He picked up a ball and said, 'Now, gentlemen, the object I'm holding is called a football. Now the object of the game is . . .

From the back came an agitated voice: 'Hang on a minute, coach! Not so fast!'

A football widow was complaining to her husband that his passion for the game was ruining their marriage. 'You never take me out,' she wailed. 'You never buy me presents. You're never at home if there's a match on anywhere. You never even remember our anniversary. Why I'll bet you've even forgotten the date of our wedding!'

'Of course I haven't!' scoffed her husband. 'It was the day Sweden beat Germany in the UEFA Under-Eighteen Championship at Lomma!'

A player was taken to hospital with a dislocated knee, incurred during a match, and his agonised roarings were heard all over casualty as the doctor tried to put the joint back into place. Said the doctor, 'For a supposedly hardened League player, you're making a hell of a lot of fuss. There's a woman next door who's having a baby and she isn't making half the fuss you're making!'

'Maybe so,' said the injured player. 'But in her case, nobody's trying to push anything back in!'

A group of supporters of the local football team
assembled outside the gates just before kick-off and
discovered that one member was missing. 'Oh, yes,
I remember,' said one of them. 'Harry said
something about getting married this afternoon at
two-thirty.'

'You must be joking!' said his neighbour. 'That
means he won't get here until half-time!'

The home captain was talking to the visiting referee. 'Now we don't expect any favouritism,' he said. 'However, I'd like to point out that our ground is next to a hospital and there's a canal over on the far side – and we haven't lost a home match all season.'

A Fourth Division goalkeeper missed a simple kick at goal and as he picked up the ball from the back of the net, a spectator shouted, 'Call yourself a goalkeeper? I could have caught that shot in me mouth!'

'So could I,' the goalkeeper yelled back, 'if my mouth was as big as yours!'

A Fourth Division team was about to play the First Division leaders in a Cup match, and the manager was giving them a last-minute pep-talk. 'All right, lads,' he said. 'Go out there and slay them! You'll be the giant-killers of the decade. And then I'll get enough money to replace the lot of you!'

A forward had a reputation for very hard play and following a match one day he returned to the dressing room with a hell of a leg on him: lacerations down the shin-bone, dislocated knee cap, bruising to the thigh and grazes everywhere. The only trouble was he didn't know who the leg belonged to.

'What did the manager say to you last Saturday when you let in three own goals?'
    'Shall I leave out the swear words?'
    'Yes.'
    'He didn't say anything.'

One Saturday morning a man was standing at the bar staring thoughtfully into his pint of beer. A friend approached and asked, 'What's bothering you, Joe? You're really deep in thought.'

'Well,' said Joe, 'this morning my wife ran away with my best friend.'

'Joe!' said his friend sympathetically. 'That's terrible!'

'It certainly is,' agreed Joe. 'It means we're short of a goalkeeper for the match this afternoon.'

England was playing Ireland and the ground was packed. There wasn't an empty seat – except for the one next to Mike Murphy. Mike's friend, Pat, tapped him on the shoulder and said, 'How come you have an empty seat beside you?'

'Oh, that was for the wife,' said Mike.

'Didn't she want to come to the match?'

'It's not that. You see, she died three days ago.'

'Oh, I am sorry,' said Pat. 'Couldn't one of your friends have come instead so as not to waste the seat?'

'Not really,' answered Mike. 'They all wanted to go to the funeral.'

Boss: 'You told me you were going to see your dentist yesterday, but I saw you at White Hart Lane with a friend.
Employee: 'That's right, sir – that was my dentist.'

The goalkeeper wasn't looking at all happy and a friend said, 'I hear you didn't do so well in goal this afternoon.'

'Listen,' said the goalkeeper. 'If I hadn't been there, we'd have lost 25–nil!'

'Oh? What was the final score then?'

'24–nil!'

A team manager came home unexpectedly one evening when a game he was due to watch was called off. He found the house in darkness, slipped in quietly, mounted the stairs and switched on the bedroom light to discover his assistant in bed with his wife. 'Tommy!' he said sadly. 'I *have* to. But you?'

There was once a manager of a small and unsuccessful Fourth Division club who had a rather inflated notion of his own prowess and leadership. He attended a convention of club managers at the Savoy Hotel and fell into conversation with a well-known sports commentator. Looking round at the assembled team bosses, he remarked, 'How many great club managers do you think there are in this room?'

'One less than you think!' replied the commentator.

A team manager was in a pub when a horse walked in and ordered a pint. They chatted and the horse revealed that he played.

'What position?' asked the manager.

'Goalkeeper,' replied the horse.

The manager invited the horse to turn out for his team. For four Saturdays the horse played and not once did the ball pass him. After the fourth game the manager said, 'You're playing brilliantly, but as we're not scoring any ourselves, I'm thinking of making you a striker.'

'But I'd have to run!' protested the horse.

'Of course you'd have to run!' said the manager.

'But I can't!' said the horse. 'If I could run, I'd be at Ascot instead of playing this stupid game!'

As the funeral procession passed along the street a passer-by noticed a pair of football boots on the coffin which was being carried by four young men. He nudged the man standing next to him and, pointing to the boots, said, 'Well-known footballer, was he?'

'Oh, no,' came the reply. 'Those belong to one of the bearers. He kicks off at two-thirty.'

For the third time in the first ten minutes of the match the referee awarded a penalty against the home team. An angry supporter shouted, 'Oi, ref, are you blind or what?'

The referee strode over to the touchline and demanded, 'What was that you said?'

'Blimey' the fan shouted back, 'Are you deaf as well?'

A disgraceful brawl took place at a recent Southern League match and a tribunal met to determine the cause. They called in the captain of the home team and said, 'Will you tell the tribunal how the fight started.'

'I didn't see any fight,' said the captain.

'You didn't? Well then tell us what you did see.'

'Well,' said the captain, 'Parker elbowed Thomas in the stomach, and as he went down, he put his hand in the mud and Bannerman stood on it. Then Parker's mate, Gibson, punched Bannerman in the mouth and knocked out a couple of teeth. Thomas got up and flattened Parker, and I could see the whole thing was probably going to turn into a fight, so I left the pitch.'

'Was there a big crowd at the match on Saturday?'

'Big crowd?' There were so few of us, the players gave us a round of applause when we walked in!'

I went to Highbury last Saturday and I've never seen so many people trying to get into a match! I said to the fellow next to me, 'Do you think we'll get in?'

He said, 'I hope so! I'm the referee!'

'It's obvious why we got beaten last Saturday. The referee comes from the same town as the visiting team.'

'Well, it's only natural, then, isn't it? He's got to travel back in the same train with them.'

A former footballer who had become rather corpulent was asked to turn out for a charity match but he refused. 'I'm so disappointed!' said the organiser. 'Won't you change your mind?'

'No, son, I won't,' said the ex-footballer. 'I tried it a few years ago. As soon as the ball came towards me, my brain rapped out all the old commands – run towards the ball at speed, trap it, beat the defender, kick for goal . . . !'

'So it's all still there, then!' said the organiser.

'No, it isn't. You see, when my brain rapped out the orders, my body said, "Who me?"'

A new amateur team had just been formed in a northern mining town. Just before their first match the team captain addressed the lads. 'Now remember, boys,' he said, 'if you don't have possession, go for their shins or their ankles. Trip 'em up, and when they're down, make sure they stay down. Now then – who's got the ball?'

'Never mind the ball,' said a voice from the back. 'Let's get on with the bloody game!'

A policeman on duty at a football ground saw a man with a gorilla walking towards him. He approached the man and said, 'Didn't I speak to you yesterday about that gorilla?'

'That's right, officer,' said the man. 'I found him wandering in the streets and I asked you what I should do with him.'

'And I told you to take it to the zoo.'

'Yes, you did, and I took him to the zoo and he enjoyed it so much, today I thought I'd bring him to a football match!'

Two fans were standing together in the pouring rain, watching the slowest game they had seen all season.

'Tell me again about all the fun we're having,' said one. 'I keep forgetting.'

First Irishman: 'There's a girl at work who's so stupid, she thinks a football coach has four wheels!'

Second Irishman: 'Would you believe that! How many wheels does it have?'

New player: 'Sorry about this afternoon, skipper. I've never played this badly before.'

Captain: 'Oh, you have played before, have you?'

The dressing room had an air of gloom and despondency about it as the captain breezed in to give his players a peptalk. 'All right, lads,' he said cheerfully, 'this is not the time to be superstitious. Just because we've lost the last twelve games doesn't necessarily mean we're going to lose today!'

'I hear your team took your 21–0 defeat last Saturday very badly.'

'Yes, they did.'

'Sad about the goalkeeper. Could some of the players not have stopped him hanging himself from the goalposts?'

'Stopped him! Who the hell do you think helped him tie the rope to the crossbar?'

'I hear your football club is looking for a treasurer.'

'That's right.'

'But didn't you take on a new treasurer last month?'

'Yes – that's the one we're looking for!'

Two men were sitting in a pub watching 'Match of the Day' on television. It was a First Division game and one of the men remarked, 'You know, the manager of the home team was trying to get me for months.'

'Was he?' said his friend. 'Who were you playing with at the time?'

'His wife!'

'Do you know,' asked the vicar, 'what happens to little boys who play football every Sunday afternoon instead of coming to Bible class?'

'Yes,' replied little Sammy. 'They grow up to play in the First Division, become international stars, appear on television, and get very, very rich!'

The Cup Final was being shown on television and a viewer was yelling and shouting as loudly as the fans at the ground. 'I can't understand what all the fuss is about,' said his wife as she handed him a cup of tea. 'I thought they decided who the champions were last year!'

A man had a son in the local team and never missed a match. However, one Saturday afternoon the team had an away match and he was unable to attend the game. He asked his son to telephone the result as soon as the game was over. When the call came through his wife picked up the telephone and after listening for a few moments, reported, 'It's Tom – he says he's had his nose broken, some teeth knocked out, and he's lost an ear!'

'Yes, yes,' said the father impatiently. 'But who won?'

The coach was tearing a strip off his star centre-half. 'Your game's gone all to hell,' he said, 'and I know the reason why. See that you stay away from women until the end of the season! Is that clear?'

'OK, OK,' said the player. 'No more dates until the end of the season.'

However, the next day the coach was walking down the street when who should he bump into but the same player with a voluptuous blonde on his arm.

'Now look,' said the player. 'Don't get excited! This lady is my wife.'

'*Your* wife!' roared the coach. 'Why you bastard – that's *my* wife!'

There was a report last week that a British underwear company brought out a new brassiere to coincide with the World Cup. They called it 'Scotland' – it had plenty of support but no cups.

Overheard in the boardroom: 'He's definitely an honest referee. When he's bought, he stays bought.'

A chap somewhat the worse for liquor staggered up to the turnstiles at a Wigan home match last Saturday. 'I'm not selling you a ticket,' said the attendant. 'You're drunk!'

'Of course I'm drunk!' said the man. 'You don't think I'd come to a Wigan match sober, do you?'

'I hear you've got a new job?'

'That's right. It's one of the easiest jobs I've ever had.'

'What do you do?'

'I keep score for Stockport County.'

A businessman came home one evening in a thoroughly bad mood. His wife asked him, 'What's got into you?'

'One of the juniors asked for the afternoon off to go to his grandmother's funeral. I thought it was the old trick to get to the football game, so I followed him.'

'Was it a good game?' asked the wife.

'Game be damned! It *was* his grandmother's funeral!'

Mother: 'Well, how did you like your visit to the British Museum with Daddy?'

Billy: 'Great! Our team won 5–3!'

It had been a bad day for the club's leading striker. Six times goals had been set up for him, and six times he had missed. As he entered the dressing room, he asked, 'Has anyone got 10p? I want to telephone a friend.'

'Here's 20p,' said the captain. 'Telephone all your friends!'

A footballer broke his leg in a home match one Saturday afternoon and had to go to hospital. A few days later one of the other players visited him. The injured footballer was by no means the team's best player, and was rather worried about losing his place on the team.

'Oh, you don't want to worry about that,' said his fellowplayer. 'Why, everyone's been talking about you. Only yesterday, the captain said, "Whatever happened to old what's-his-name?" '

Punter: '£50 on Liverpool to beat Dundee.'

Bookie: 'Sorry – we don't take bets on friendlies.'

Punter: 'Don't be daft! Liverpool don't play
friendlies!'

A famous football coach was finishing his
pep-talk to the team just before an important
match. 'Remember, men,' he said, 'football builds
leadership, initiative and individuality! Now get out
on to that field and do exactly as I've told you!'

'What happens exactly at a football match?'

'Well, two teams of eleven players each go on to a large field and they try to kick a ball into a net while another person, called a referee, watches them.'

'What happens when the referee isn't watching them?'

'Well, then they kick each other.'

A fan took his girlfriend to a game for the first time. She couldn't understand what was going on at all and had no idea about the functions of each player. 'What's that man doing standing at the big net?' she asked.

'He's the goalkeeper,' said her boyfriend. 'He has to make sure that the ball doesn't go into the net.'

'And how much does he get for that?'

'Oh, I don't know – about £200,000 a year.'

'Good gracious,' said the young lady. 'Wouldn't it be cheaper to have it boarded up?'

Woody had played like a hairy goat all afternoon. When the team came off the ground after the final whistle, he said sheepishly to the coach, 'Sorry about that. I'm not playing my usual game today.'

'What game is that then?' said the coach. 'Croquet?'

'That new centre-forward is a steady player, isn't he.'

'Steady? If he was any steadier, he'd be motionless.'

There was a report in the paper last week about a young man who won £250,000 on the football pools. Apparently he had told his mother and father that he was generously going to give them £50 each out of his winnings. The old couple were so upset that the father confessed that they were not the young man's real parents. 'What!' he yelled. 'Are you telling me that I'm a bastard?'

'You are that,' said his father. 'And a damn mean one at that!'

Tall spectator at football match: 'What a crowd! Why, there must be 30,000 people watching the game this afternoon!'

Small spectator standing behind him: 'Well, let's just say 29,999!'

A soccer fan has been defined as someone sitting several hundred feet from the ball who can see it better than the referee standing right next to it.

A team manager was talking to a young man who wanted to become a professional footballer. 'You must understand,' he said, 'that if you want to be a really good footballer, the best thing is to give up smoking, drinking and girls.'

'I see,' said the young man thoughtfully. 'Tell me, what's the next best thing?'

First girl: 'I hear your Joe's joined United. What position does he play?'

Second girl: 'I'm not sure but I heard some of the other players say he was their main drawback.'

Striker: 'Sorry about missing that last goal, chief. I know it was an easy one, and believe me, I could kick myself.'

Coach: 'I shouldn't bother. You'd probably miss.'

The referee rushed over to where the player was writing on the ground just outside the penalty area. 'Did you see who it was that hit you?' he asked.

'No,' groaned the player. 'But I got a note of his number.'

'Aren't you going to the Bradford City match this Saturday?'

'Why the hell should I? They didn't come to see me when I was bad!'

The selection committee members were discussing the performances of their players. 'Now we come to the goalkeeper, Nick Fanshawe,' said the chairman. 'What are your views on him?'

'As a goalkeeper,' snorted one member, 'I think Venus de Milo could do a better job!'

After a disastrous game the coach got stuck into one of the worst offenders. 'Fosdyke, you're playing like an old woman! You should be ashamed of yourself! You're useless – a liability to the team!'

After the coach had left, one of Fosdyke's mates tried to console him. 'Don't take any notice of the coach,' he said comfortingly. 'He only repeats what he hears everyone else saying.'

A young Crystal Palace defender had been playing badly all season. Deciding it was time to pull his socks up, he went out one Saturday afternoon and gave it all he'd got. Proud of his efforts, he sought out the coach after the game and asked, 'Well, coach have you noticed any improvement in me since last week?'

The coach looked at him for a moment and then said, 'You've had a haircut!'

An ex-player was holding forth in his local to a group of hangers-on. 'When I was playing professionally,' he said, 'I helped Manchester United beat Leeds for three seasons running.'

'Really?' said one listener. 'Which side were you playing for?'

'I hear you were playing football last Sunday, my son.'

'That right, vicar. It's not a sin to play football on the Sabbath, is it?'

'It is, the way you play it.'

WALKING IN CYPRUS

44 WALKS IN THE SOUTH AND THE NORTH

About the Author

Nike and Jacint met many years ago on a long coach journey as they both travelled into the unknown to build a new life in a different country. It wasn't long before they became inseparable. Travelling quickly emerged as their favourite activity: they had their first walking holiday in Madeira in 2008 and now wherever they go they try to find the best trails. When they first visited Cyprus they were mesmerised by the diverse scenery, but discovered that information about trails was difficult to find and walking maps were not available. Having collected the best routes, they want to share their passion for walking on this fascinating island with others.

Nike went to journalism school and Jacint is a keen photographer. In 2016 they moved from London to Surrey where they can enjoy the countryside and hills.

WALKING IN CYPRUS

44 WALKS IN THE SOUTH AND THE NORTH

by Nike Werstroh and Jacint Mig

JUNIPER HOUSE, MURLEY MOSS,
OXENHOLME ROAD, KENDAL, CUMBRIA LA9 7RL
www.cicerone.co.uk

© Nike Werstroh and Jacint Mig 2017
First edition 2017
ISBN: 978 1 85284 837 8

Printed by KHL Printing, Singapore
A catalogue record for this book is available from the British Library.
All photographs are by the authors unless otherwise stated.

Route mapping by Lovell Johns www.lovelljohns.com
Contains OpenStreetMap.org data © OpenStreetMap
contributors, CC-BY-SA. NASA relief data courtesy of ESRI

*In memory of Nike's Grandma, who would have been
proud to see this book.*

Acknowledgements

A special thank you to Alison Currier who read most of the walks, and to the Hall family who, inspired by our enthusiastic talks about Cyprus, visited the island and tried some of the trails. A big thank you to Jonathan Williams of Cicerone for giving us the opportunity to discover and collect Cyprus' trails.

Updates to this Guide

While every effort is made by our authors to ensure the accuracy of guidebooks as they go to print, changes can occur during the lifetime of an edition. Any updates that we know of for this guide will be on the Cicerone website (www.cicerone.co.uk/837/updates), so please check before planning your trip. We also advise that you check information about such things as transport, accommodation and shops locally. Even rights of way can be altered over time.

The route maps in this guide are derived from publicly-available data, databases and crowd-sourced data. As such they have not been through the detailed checking procedures that would generally be applied to a published map from an official mapping agency, although naturally we have reviewed them closely in the light of local knowledge as part of the preparation of this guide.

We are always grateful for information about any discrepancies between a guidebook and the facts on the ground, sent by email to updates@cicerone.co.uk or by post to Cicerone, Juniper House, Murley Moss, Oxenholme Road, Kendal LA9 7RL, United Kingdom.

Register your book: To sign up to receive free updates, special offers and GPX files where available, register your book at www.cicerone.co.uk.

Front cover: View of the Madari ridge from Mnimata Piskopon Trail (Walk 13)

CONTENTS

Symbols used on route maps

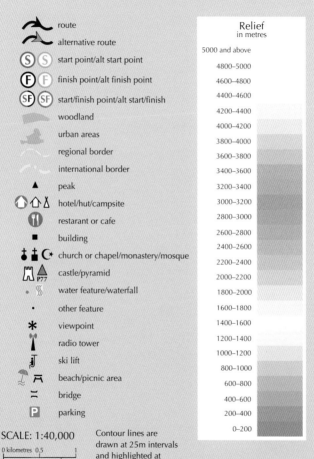

	route
	alternative route
S S	start point/alt start point
F F	finish point/alt finish point
SF SF	start/finish point/alt start/finish
	woodland
	urban areas
	regional border
	international border
▲	peak
⌂ ⌂ ⅄	hotel/hut/campsite
	restarant or cafe
■	building
♱ ♱ ☪	church or chapel/monastery/mosque
	castle/pyramid
∘ ⧘	water feature/waterfall
•	other feature
✳	viewpoint
	radio tower
	ski lift
☂ ⊼	beach/picnic area
∸	bridge
P	parking

Relief
in metres

5000 and above
4800–5000
4600–4800
4400–4600
4200–4400
4000–4200
3800–4000
3600–3800
3400–3600
3200–3400
3000–3200
2800–3000
2600–2800
2400–2600
2200–2400
2000–2200
1800–2000
1600–1800
1400–1600
1200–1400
1000–1200
800–1000
600–800
400–600
200–400
0–200

SCALE: 1:40,000

0 kilometres 0.5   1

0 miles   0.5

Contour lines are drawn at 25m intervals and highlighted at 100m intervals.

GPX files

GPX files for all routes can be downloaded free at www.cicerone.co.uk/837/GPX .

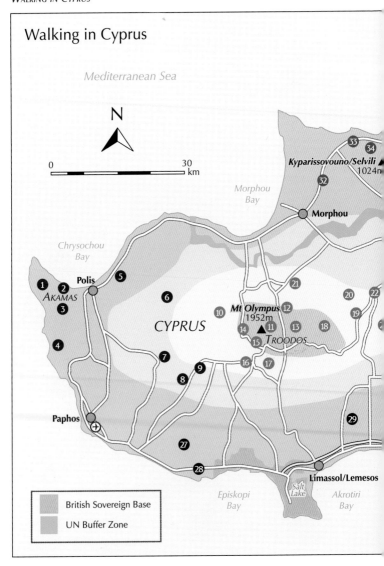

Walking in Cyprus

Mediterranean Sea

N

0   30
km

Morphou Bay

Kyparissovouno/Selvili ▲
1024m

㉝ ㉞

㉜

Morphou

Chrysochou Bay

① ② **Polis** ⑤
AKAMAS
③

⑥

⑩ **Mt Olympus** ⑫
     1952m

㉑

⑳ ㉒

④

CYPRUS

⑭ ▲ ⑪ ⑬ ⑱ ⑲
⑮ *TROODOS*

⑦

⑧ ⑨

⑯ ⑰

Paphos
⊕

㉙

㉗

㉘

Limassol/Lemesos

| | British Sovereign Base |
| | UN Buffer Zone |

Episkopi Bay

Salt Lake

Akrotiri Bay

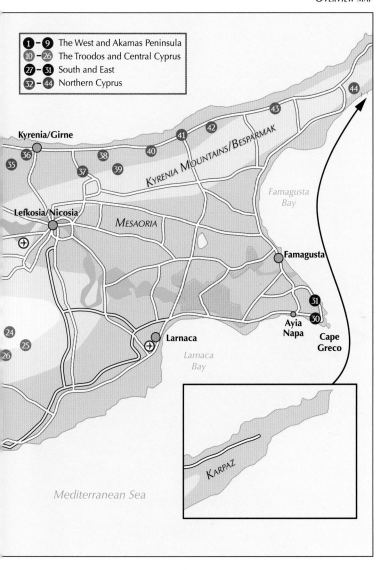

1 – 9 The West and Akamas Peninsula
10 – 26 The Troodos and Central Cyprus
27 – 31 South and East
32 – 44 Northern Cyprus

Kyrenia/Girne

KYRENIA MOUNTAINS/BESPARMAK

Famagusta Bay

Lefkosia/Nicosia

MESAORIA

Famagusta

Ayia Napa

Cape Greco

Larnaca

Larnaca Bay

KARPAZ

Mediterranean Sea

The narrowest section of the Avakas gorge (Walk 4)

INTRODUCTION

According to legend, the goddess of love and beauty, Aphrodite, was born in Cyprus. Her birthplace, Petra tou Romiou – the famous rock formation near Paphos/Baf – rising from the turquoise sea, attracts many tourists every day. Admiring the striking sea stack from the pebbly beach in the early hours before the coachloads of noisy tourists arrive, you can see why a goddess of beauty would rise from the sea on that very spot. Cyprus has a strong connection with Greek mythology, and today places of interest and even walking trails bear the names of mythological figures.

The scenery changes from the rugged coastline of the Akamas Peninsula, washed with turquoise water, to the wildflower-carpeted meadows and pine-covered slopes of Troodos; across the cultivated Mesaoria Plains to the narrow, serene Kyrenia/Beşparmak mountains. The Kyrenia range leads to the Karpaz/Karpass Peninsula, which is like an outstretched arm pointing towards Turkey.

Sunshine, a Mediterranean climate and golden beaches with crystal-clear waters have attracted tourists for many years. But walkers – who prefer to leave the hustle of seaside towns, noisy taverns and the busy archaeological sites behind – have only just started to discover

Aphrodite's birthplace, Petra tou Romiou

The Profitis Elias chapel among the vineyards near Pano Panagia (Walk 7)

Cyprus' outstanding walking trails. The sound of waves crashing against the rocks and the smell of seawater accompany the walker on sunny coastal trails, while birdsong entertains them as they walk through the dramatic Avakas Gorge on the Akamas Peninsula. Hikers might spot shy mouflon (a type of wild sheep) hopping skilfully on the steep slopes in Paphos Forest and the wild donkeys staring curiously at people on the Karpaz/Karpass Peninsula.

In the centre of the island, in the Troodos mountains, zigzagging footpaths lead to small, hidden churches and Byzantine monasteries – many of which are on the UNESCO Word Heritage List for their unique architecture and colourful frescos. Winding nature trails on pine-covered slopes with stunning views give walkers the

opportunity to admire the beauty of these mountains.

Meanwhile, with castles proudly perched on rocks and mysterious monasteries in the shade of mighty trees, the thin, dramatic Kyrenia mountain range stretches across almost the entire length of Northern Cyprus.

In every season the island has its own magic to share with visitors. In some winters, snow covers the mountain peaks of Troodos, and Cyprus has Europe's most southerly ski resort. In spring, streams grow wider and colourful wildflowers carpet the meadows, while in the peak of summer the hazy air is filled with the chirping of cicadas. In autumn, families gather together to harvest grapes that grow on sunny slopes. At any time of the year elderly people are often found gossiping in front of their homes on the narrow streets of peaceful villages.

After a day spent exploring the trails, walkers might enjoy a well-deserved dinner in a rustic restaurant in one of the seaside towns or villages. Cypriot cuisine is strongly related to Greek and Turkish cuisine but with a local twist; fresh vegetables, olives, halloumi cheese, meat, fish and Greek yoghurt are among the ingredients common to traditional Cypriot food. Wine is a necessary accompaniment for local dishes, and in Cyprus people have been making it for thousands of years. Commandaria, the sweet dessert wine, is believed to be the oldest named wine in the world: it was served at the wedding of Richard the Lionheart in Limassol and the king was so impressed that he pronounced Commandaria 'the wine of kings and the king of wines'.

Due to its location, the island played a significant role in trading from around 3000BC and through the medieval centuries. It has belonged to different empires in its eventful past, with numerous artefacts and remains of ancient buildings around the island attesting to its diverse culture and troubled history. However, unlike other Mediterranean islands, it is not only the distant past that has left its legacy: after the island gained independence in 1960, tensions between the Greek and Turkish Cypriot communities grew, resulting in an eventual coup by the Greek Cypriots and an invasion by Turkey. The UN-controlled buffer zone (known as the 'Green Line') that runs like a long scar across the island, dividing its inhabitants, demonstrates that the recent past is still affecting the lives of many in Cyprus. This, as well as the island's earlier history, is described further in 'Brief history'.

However, while Cyprus may be politically divided, the amazing scenery can be enjoyed on both sides of the island regardless of political views. Cypriots – whether they speak Greek or Turkish, attend church or mosque – greet visitors with a friendly welcome on both sides of the Green Line.

LOCATION AND GEOGRAPHY

Cyprus, surrounded by three continents, lies in the north eastern corner of the Mediterranean Sea. It is only 74km south of Turkey, about 100km from Syria and approximately 800km from mainland Greece. The island is 240km long and 100km wide at its widest point. It is the third largest island in the Mediterranean Sea, from which it rose millions of years ago.

The foundation rocks of Cyprus were once part of the oceanic crust of the Tethys Ocean and as such weren't connected to any continental plate. In the late Miocene period, the African Plate levered the floor of the Tethys Ocean, causing Cyprus to emerge. The Troodos mountains were once part of the ocean bed and today they form the best-preserved example of ocean floor on the Earth's surface.

Here geologists can study the prehistoric sea floor.

Cyprus's two mountain ranges – the Troodos and the Kyrenia mountains – dominate its landscape. Troodos, located in the middle of the island, is mainly formed of igneous rock with its lower slopes covered by chalk. The Kyrenia, running across nearly the entire northern part of the island, consists of limestone and marble. About two million years ago the Kyrenia and Troodos mountains were islands; the land was constantly rising and the area between the two mountain ranges became the Mesaoria Plain.

PLANTS AND FLOWERS

There are approximately 1800 identified plant species on the island, of which around 140 are endemic. Some of the endemic plants' habitats are restricted to specific areas such as the Troodos mountains or the Akamas Peninsula.

Calabrian pine (*Pinus brutia*) forest, which thrives from sea level to an altitude of 1400m, covers the slopes of the Troodos and Kyrenia mountains and part of the Akamas Peninsula.

In Troodos the golden oak (*Quercus alnifolia*) appears at around 700m and the black pine (*Pinus nigra*) grows at higher altitudes. The Cyprus cedar (*Cedrus brevifolia*) can only be found in the Paphos Forest – especially around Trypilos Mountain. Cypress, juniper, alder and plane trees are quite common on the island.

The carob tree (*Ceratonia siliqua*) is typical to the Mediterranean region and has been used in many different ways since ancient times. It can be found growing in the wild but is widely cultivated for its edible pods. The word 'carat' – the unit used to measure the purity of gold – is derived from the Greek word *keration* as the pods' small seeds were used to measure gold in ancient times.

Colourful wildflowers begin to bloom from late February and the meadows can be carpeted with flowers well into May. Walking is the best way to observe the flowers, and even

The Italian orchid (Orchis italica) – or as it is commonly known, the 'naked man orchid' – is native to the Mediterranean region

without specialist knowledge you can admire the extensive colours. Rock roses – their colours ranging from white and yellow to pink – often cover the hillsides.

The Kyrenia mountains are home to many wildflowers, including orchids. The greatest number of wild orchids appear in March and April. More than 30 species of orchid can be found in Cyprus, in places ranging from shady forest floors to rocky hillsides. The Cyprus bee orchid and the Lapithos bee orchid are endemic.

The island's national flower, the Cyprus cyclamen (*Cyclamen cyprium*), which blooms pink or white, flowers in the early autumn in moist forests. The dark-coloured, protected Cyprus tulip (*Tulipa cypria*) grows in the Akamas Peninsula, the Kormakitis/Kormacit Peninsula and in some parts of the Kyrenia range. The St Hilarion cabbage (*Brassica hilarionis*) can be found mainly in Northern Cyprus, especially near St Hilarion Castle (Walk 36).

Typical plants and flowers are labelled on most nature trails in Southern Cyprus, so walkers can learn to recognise them.

WILDLIFE

There are 21 known species of mammal on the island. Only the luckiest walkers will spot the biggest of these – the shy Cypriot mouflon – hopping on the steep slopes in the less busy areas of the Paphos Forest and the mountains of Troodos. There is, however, a mouflon enclosure at Stavros Tis Psokas in Paphos Forest, providing an opportunity to see these endemic animals.

Mouflon once populated the mountains of Cyprus in greater numbers, but by the middle of the 20th century hunting had decreased this population significantly. Then in 1939 the whole Paphos Forest was designated a Game Protected Area, and today it is also a Special Protected Area; thanks to these great efforts to protect the mouflon and their habitat, their numbers have increased to a satisfactory level.

Further north, dark-coloured wild donkeys inhabit the Karpaz/Karpass Peninsula. These animals are descendants of the domesticated donkeys abandoned by people who were displaced by political conflict in the 1970s (see 'Brief history').

Two bird species – the Cyprus warbler and Cyprus wheatear – are only found in Cyprus, and there is a conservation project in place to protect the endangered Griffon vulture.

Due to its geographic location, Cyprus is an important stopping place for migrating birds, and is therefore a great place for birdwatching. Unfortunately, despite the activity being outlawed in 1974, many birds are illegally trapped, killed and served as a delicacy in some restaurants.

Some of the sandy beaches on the island are important hatching places for the green turtle and the loggerhead turtle – both of which are endangered and protected. Turtles lay eggs every 2–5 years on the same beach where they were born, and development of the beaches means that the adult turtle might be unable to return to its birthplace. Tourism, fishing and pollution have decreased the number of suitable nesting beaches around the island, but there is now a great effort to protect the areas where the turtles lay their eggs. Hatcheries at Lara Beach in South Cyprus and Alagadi Beach in North Cyprus are specially protected areas where visitors can learn about turtles and the effort to safeguard them. In North Cyprus the Marine Turtle Research Group has been monitoring nestling turtles since 1992.

A very small number of monk seals is believed to be living on Cyprus' remote shores. (It is estimated that there are fewer than 700 monk seals in the entire Mediterranean.)

Most of the snakes in Cyprus are harmless; however the blunt-nosed viper is venomous but it only attacks in self-defence. Its body is about 1.5m long, silvery-beige in colour with rectangular markings and black spots on its head. It is usually found near water. If bitten by one of these, seek medical help immediately: call 112 or go to one of the hospitals or medical centres in the towns.

The 2m-long large whipsnake, which is shiny and black, is aggressive but non-venomous; however its bite is painful so keep your distance.

Also common – on the coastlines and the mountains of North Cyprus – is the light-brown coin snake. There are dark coin-shaped patterns

The whipsnake's bite is painful but non-venomous

along its body and it can grow up to 1.7m. It might be aggressive but is non-venomous.

BRIEF HISTORY

Cyprus' eventful past, from ancient times right through the 20th century, could fill this book. This section gives only a very brief history, highlighting the key events which have shaped the Cyprus we see today.

The island has belonged to a number of different empires over the centuries, with each having an influence on its culture, architecture, cuisine and religion. This is very much in evidence on the walks, where you'll come across ruins, Byzantine churches, Venetian bridges, monasteries, castles and EOKA (National Organisation of Cypriot Fighters) hideouts.

Early history

There is evidence that Cyprus has been inhabited since 8000BC. Today, the ruins of city kingdoms in Kourion, Paphos, Soloi, Lapithos/Lapta and Salamis – each dating to different periods in the island's ancient history – are well visited by tourists.

The name 'Cyprus' means copper, and refers to the fact that copper was abundant here, however it is unknown whether the island was named after the metal or the metal after the island. In earlier times the metallic copper was found on the surface. Copper was reduced to metal

as pine resins in groundwater mixed with copper sulphate. Cyprus supplied the ancient world with weapons-grade copper, which was used to make swords and shields. When the copper was no longer to be found on the surface, Cypriots discovered that if cuprous earth and umber were mixed and then heated, they could get melted copper. Smelting began in 2760BC. Cyprus was an ideal place for mining and smelting as the island had all the necessary natural resources. The forests provided wood to fire the furnaces: they had to be replanted to meet demand, but the rainfall in the mountains made cultivation possible. Copper has been mined on Cyprus for 4000 years, producing millions of tons of slag. This used to be used to build roads but today the slag-heaps are protected monuments.

Cyprus was part of the Persian Empire and was only released from it in 333BC with Alexander the Great's victory over the Persian ruler Darius III. The island then became part of the Greek Empire. When Alexander died in 323BC, Cyprus was taken over by Egypt and became part of the Hellenistic Egypt under Ptolemy I, and the island's capital was moved from Salamis to Paphos.

In 58BC the Roman Empire annexed Cyprus and the following 600 years passed under Roman rule. There are many ruins of buildings and mosaics from this period which can still be seen today, such as the mosaics excavated at the Paphos

Dramatic view of the Kyrenia range from Buffavento Castle (Walk 37)

Archaeological Site by the harbour of Kato Paphos.

Christianity appeared on the island in AD45 when Apostle Paul started spreading the new religion. The Church of Cyprus was set up by apostles and Cyprus became 'the Island of Saints'.

When the Roman Empire was divided in AD395, Cyprus came under the eastern half – the Byzantine Empire. During the Byzantine period (4th–12th century), many impressive churches were built and remarkable frescos were painted, such as at Agios Nikolaos tis Stegis (Walk 12), Asinou church (Walk 21) and Panagia tou Araka church (Walk 22).

The growing Islamic empire started to attack Byzantine lands in the 7th century; Cyprus, located between the two empires, was also attacked and many coastal settlements were destroyed in AD647. Castles and fortifications were built to protect the land from Arab attacks, and the ruins of St Hilarion, Buffavento and Kantara castles (Walks 36, 37 and 43) in the Kyrenia mountains are still visited by many.

The Middle Ages

On his third crusade, between 1189 and 1192, bad weather forced Richard the Lionheart's fleet to dock in Limassol. There, Isaak Komninos – emperor of Cyprus at the time – tried to capture King Richard's fiancée, Berengaria of Navarre, and his sister. In response, King Richard marched on Limassol and Komninos fled to Kantara Castle. In 1191 Richard married Berengaria in Limassol Castle, and Cyprus became the only foreign country where an English royal wedding was held.

Richard stayed in Cyprus for a year and during that time he conquered the entire island and then sold it to the Knights Templar. However, the Knights couldn't afford to keep the island and in turn sold it to Guy de Lusignan in 1192. From then until 1474 Cyprus was ruled by Lusignan descendants. Bellapais Abbey and many other splendid buildings were built during this period.

The last Lusignan king, James II, married a Venetian noblewoman who handed Cyprus over to Venice. The island was under Venetian rule from 1489 to 1571. Cyprus played an important role for the Venetians as a trading route and was used as a defence against the threatening Ottoman Empire. Forts were built around the big cities such as Famagusta/Mağusa and Nicosia/Lefkoşa.

In 1570–71 Famagusta was attacked by the Ottomans and a year later the city fell. With this, a new era began in the island's history: Turkish settlers arrived on the island and for almost 300 years Cyprus was controlled by the Ottomans.

While the Ottomans left the Greek orthodox churches intact, they converted some of the Gothic Catholic churches into mosques – for example the Lala Mustafa Pasha mosque in Famagusta – and their influence on the culture and architecture of the island is still very much in evidence.

20th century

The origin of the campaign for *enosis* (union with Greece) can be traced back to the Greek War of Independence (1821–32) when the Greeks fought for their independence

Roudia Bridge, built by the Venetians, connects the two banks of the Xeros River (Walk 9)

19

from the Ottoman Empire. Some Greek Cypriots also rebelled, but the Ottomans executed 486 Greek Cypriots – accused of conspiring with the Greeks – on 9 July 1821. The desire to become part of Greece grew stronger when Greece became independent in 1830, but Cyprus remained under Ottoman control until 1878, when it came under British control. The British assumed administrative responsibility while Turkey maintained sovereignty, then at the beginning of WWI Great Britain annexed Cyprus and from 1925 the island was a Crown Colony.

The Greek Cypriots had hoped that British control would eventually help them achieve enosis. However, impatience grew and the Ethniki Organosi tou Kyprakou Agona (EOKA – National Organisation of Cypriot Fighters) was founded with the intention of ending British rule and achieving enosis. Between 1955 and 1958 EOKA carried out a series of attacks on the British military.

Turkish Cypriots only comprised a 17% minority of the population and they feared that if Cyprus achieved a union with Greece they would be excluded. Therefore they demanded *taksim* (partition), to divide the island between Greece and Turkey.

In 1960 Cyprus finally became independent, with Archbishop Makarios III becoming the first president of the Republic of Cyprus, but in 1963 serious violence broke out and the tensions between Greek and Turkish Cypriots increased. In 1964 a UN peacekeeping force arrived in Cyprus. Major General Peter Young drew a green line on the map, dividing the capital, Nicosia, between the Greek and Turkish. This later became known as the 'Green Line' and went on to divide the whole island.

In 1974 the Greek Cypriots, supported by the military junta in Greece, carried out a coup. In response, Turkey invaded the island. By 16 August 1974 the northern part – 37% of the island – was controlled by Turkey. The 190,000 Greek Cypriots that lived in the northern areas left their homes and lost their land and businesses as they fled to the south. Meanwhile, 50,000 Turkish Cypriots moved from the south to Northern Cyprus. A number of people were killed and many disappeared during the conflict, and the UN has controlled and patrolled the Green Line – which runs across the entire island – ever since.

In 1983 the Turkish Republic of Northern Cyprus – a self-declared state recognised only by Turkey – was announced. In 2003, for the first time in almost 30 years, the border was opened, allowing Cypriots to visit the opposing parts. Since then several border crossing points have been opened, allowing Cypriots and tourists to travel around the island.

Cyprus joined the European Union as a de facto divided island in 2004. The whole of Cyprus is EU territory and Turkish Cypriots are classed as EU citizens as they are citizens of the Republic of Cyprus (an EU country) despite the fact that they live in a part of Cyprus that is not under the Republic's government control. Since 2008 Southern Cyprus' currency has been the euro, while in Northern Cyprus it is the Turkish *lira*. Today, Nicosia is the last divided capital in Europe.

RELIGION

Most Greek Cypriots (who make up nearly 80% of the island's population) belong to the Orthodox Church of Cyprus, while most Turkish Cypriots are Sunni Muslims.

The Church of Cyprus is an autocephalous Greek Orthodox Church – meaning it has its own independent head bishop who does not report to any higher human authority. It is one of the oldest churches of this type. Ten of the churches built during the Byzantine period in the Troodos mountains are on the World Heritage List. Their steep-pitched wooden roofs are typical of the Troodos region, and some of the churches – for example Agios Nikolaos tis Tegis near Kakopetria – also have a second timber roof. The UNESCO-listed Byzantine churches are also known for their frescos; some of them – such as Asinou church near Nikitari – have their entire interior covered in these paintings.

Monasteries were generally built in the mountains, so that the monks who lived in them could be further from temptation and closer to God. Many of these buildings also contain great collections of frescos. When visiting a monastery or church in Cyprus, wear long trousers and cover your arms. Some monasteries have a selection of robes by the entrance for visitors to cover themselves up with.

When Cyprus fell under the Ottoman Empire in 1571, Turkish settlers arrived onto the island and brought their religion, Islam, with them. During the Ottoman period some churches were converted into mosques (for example the Lala Mustafa Pasha Mosque in Famagusta), creating unique and impressive constructions. These – especially the ones in Nicosia and Famagusta – can be visited by tourists. You will have to leave your shoes by the door and women have to cover their head with a headscarf. Many well-visited mosques offer headscarves for female visitors.

Although the Turkish Cypriots in Northern Cyprus are Sunni Muslims, most of them don't follow their religion too strictly; they consume alcohol and women don't cover their heads in public.

GETTING THERE

There are plenty of direct flights from UK and many other European airports to Paphos and Larnaca/Larnaka in the south of the island. Shop around for the best deals. You could also check out the well-known tour operators;

View from the section between Kionia picnic site and Machairas Monastery (Walk 24)

they offer package holidays, mainly for tourist resorts, but it's possible to book flights only with them. Easyjet, Ryanair, British Airways, Jet2 and Thomas Cook all have direct flights from UK airports.

There are no direct flights to the northern part of Cyprus. Flights arriving at Ercan – the airport in Northern Cyprus – must travel via Turkey. If you choose this option you might face a longer travelling time. If you leave the airport you need a visa to enter Turkey; this can be obtained by completing an electronic application form. You don't need a visa if you hold a British or EU passport and are only changing flights in Turkey. If you're not a British passport holder, see www.mfa.gov.tr for visa requirements for Turkey and http://mfa.gov.ct.tr for Northern Cyprus.

For the fastest possible route to the north of the island, fly to Larnaca from where border crossing points are easily accessed. From the airport you can take one of the buses to Nicosia where you can cross the border on foot.

Ferries operate between Kyrenia/ Girne and mainland Turkey – see Appendix B for booking details.

BORDER CROSSINGS

The northern part of the island – the Turkish Republic of Northern Cyprus – is a self-declared state recognised only by Turkey. It is referred to as 'Northern Cyprus' by most outsiders, but the Greek Cypriots in the south consider it an occupied area. Since 2003 Cypriots from both sides have been allowed to visit the opposing parts, and tourists can easily visit both parts of the island.

Most tourists visit South Cyprus, but for walkers there are some peaceful and spectacular walking trails to be discovered in the north. However, to get there you might need a bit more planning (see 'Getting there', above). EU passport holders don't need a visa to enter Northern Cyprus; some travel websites suggest that on entering Northern Cyprus it is necessary to fill out a form which is then stamped, but in 2016 there was no such form and it was only necessary to show passports.

There are several crossing points on the island. These are known by many different names, as Turkish, Greek and occasionally English place names are used, and they are also often referred to by the name of the nearest village. You can cross from the south to the north and vice versa on foot in Nicosia, at Ledra Palace Hotel and Ledra Street. There are five other crossing points: Limnitis/Yesilirmak, Astromeritis/Zodhia, Agios Dometios/Metehan and Pyla/Beyarmudu, Strovilia/Akyar.

The busy Ledra Street in Nicosia, lined with shops, cafés and restaurants, comes abruptly to the border crossing point. After presenting your passport to the two authorities you can continue on the very same street, but with a very different ambience. Many tourists visit both parts of the divided capital on the same day. If you want to continue towards the north, you can find minibuses departing to Kyrenia from North Nicosia just outside the old city walls. Many car hire companies offer a pick-up service

There are plenty of small waterfalls to enjoy on Walk 16

if you decide to cross the border on foot, and taxis are also available.

Some car hire companies allow you to take a car hired in the south to the northern part of the island, but extra insurance will have to be purchased. However, cars hired on the north cannot be taken to the south.

GETTING AROUND

Buses

If you want to get around by bus you need careful planning. There are buses running along the coast and serving some villages from Paphos, Limassol, Nicosia and Polis, but you need to check the timetables very carefully when planning a walk. Some villages are only served by one or two buses daily and a return journey can also be tricky. Check routes and timetables at the local bus stations and tourist offices before setting off for a walk.

Intercity buses connect major towns; for more information visit the town's bus terminal. You could also consult the local websites, but remember to check when they were last updated:

www.kapnosairportshuttle.com
www.intercity-buses.com
www.pafosbuses.com
www.cyprusbybus.com
www.limassolairportexpress.eu
www.limassolbuses.com

Buses in Northern Cyprus run between the major towns, and white minibuses, known as *dolmuş*, serve North Nicosia, Famagusta and Kyrenia. Getting around by dolmuş is cheap but they don't have a timetable; people either have to wave them down or board the vehicle at its departing point.

Bear in mind that many of the walks described in this guide start and/ or finish in a remote place with no public transport, in which case a taxi or hired car may be the only option.

Taxis and car hire

While it may seem like a disadvantage to have a car parked at one end of a linear walk, most of the time it is possible to retrace your steps or arrange a pick-up service at the other end. This also applies if you're relying on buses, as you might get to the beginning of the linear route relatively easily but then need to call a taxi at the end of the walk. In the Troodos mountains you can find taxis in Platres and Troodos Square, and it is recommended to arrange the taxi before you start your walk.

Hiring a car is easy; cars can be booked in advance or are available in towns and are very reasonably priced. On Cyprus, drive on the left. Main roads are in good condition but you can easily find yourself driving on winding, single-lane roads with the threat of rock fall. Check with your car hire company about any rules for driving on dirt roads.

If you hire a car in the south, you might be able to take it to the northern part of the island but you will need to purchase extra insurance. However, if you hire a car in the north you are not permitted to take it to the south.

Roads might be busy around the coastal towns and near the historical sights but many mountain roads are quiet. The driving habits in Cyprus may seem a bit more chaotic than in the UK, but locals know their roads and cars and they can recognise tourists on the road so driving is as safe as anywhere can ever be. A hire car is one of the best and easiest ways to get around the island.

ACCOMMODATION

Choice of accommodation is always a personal one, taking into account your budget and preferences. There are plenty of hotels and self-catering options to choose from in coastal areas, and there is a range of options both in the Troodos and further north around Kyrenia.

As a walker you might opt to tackle several day trips in the same area, or you might consider splitting your holiday between different bases. If you decide to stay in one base, for example in a coastal town, you can still enjoy different areas on the island as many places are easily reached in a day trip. When choosing accommodation you might want to bear in mind that many towns have interesting sights that you can explore after your walk.

There are also some campsites on the island; a list of Cyprus Tourism Organisation (CTO) licensed campsites can be found at www.visitcyprus.com.

A view over Ayia Eirini (Walk 20)

The vertical sea cliffs near Pissouri (Walk 28)

For accommodation resources, see Appendix B.

TOURIST INFORMATION

The tourist information offices in Limassol, Polis, Platres, Paphos, Larnaca airport, and Agia Napa provide really useful information about trails and historical sites. Booklets about the most popular nature trails and the E4 long-distance trail (which was extended onto Cyprus in 2005) are also available from the Troodos Visitor Centre; some of them can be downloaded from the Department of Forests website: www.moa.gov.cy/moa/fd/fd.nsf (select the English-language option, if required, and then 'Informative Leaflets'). Check the opening times of the Troodos Visitor Centre as it varies.

It is best to ask for information about transport at the local bus terminals and Cyprus Tourism Organisation (CTO) offices.

In Northern Cyprus there are tourist information offices in Kyrenia, Nicosia, Famagusta and Ercan airport. There is also a kiosk with maps and leaflets at the Ledra Street border crossing in Nicosia. Booklets of some of the trails, with basic maps and historical sites, are available in English.

You can also find useful information on the following websites:

www.visitcyprus.com
www.mytroodos.com
www.aboutcyprus.org.cy

and for Northern Cyprus

www.visitnorthcyprus.com
www.welcometonorthcyprus.org
www.turkishcyprus.com

LANGUAGE

Greek and Turkish are the two official languages in Cyprus, and English is widely spoken. Signs are usually in Greek, and English is in use in the south; however spelling with the Latin alphabet is not consistent. Names of places, villages, nature trails and historical sites are spelled in many different ways. Signs are in Turkish in the north but they might include the old Greek name as well. See 'Using this guide' for details of the way in which place names are presented in this guide.

WHEN TO GO AND WHAT TO TAKE

Cyprus might seem like a year-round destination, but the best times for walking are the spring and autumn months. The summer months – from May to September – are generally too hot for walking, although some of the trails in the cooler Troodos mountains might be considered. In autumn, although the land may be parched after the summer heat, there is scope for enjoying a much wider range of walks. Most rainfall occurs during winter, when snow can cover the Troodos. Perhaps the best time to discover the trails of Cyprus is the spring months, when wildflowers carpet the meadows and the temperature is warm but not too hot.

When preparing for a walk described in this book, pack what you would normally take for a day walk. Carry a waterproof jacket as showers can surprise you even in the spring (especially in the Kyrenia mountains). Take a jumper with you; Troodos is traditionally cooler than the coast. Comfortable hiking boots, sun cream and sun hat are all essential, and always carry ample water for your day.

MAPS AND WAYMARKING

Walking maps are not available for Cyprus. There are some tourist maps, which you can pick up at the airports or in the tourist offices, but they don't outline the trails. There are

publications of some of the popular trails of Northern Cyprus, including sketch maps, which are available from tourist offices. You can also pick up leaflets of the popular nature trails from tourist information offices in the south. Road maps for both parts of the island are available from tourist offices and airports.

The diverse trails in South Cyprus range from rugged coastline to forest walks, a stroll between vineyards to walking in the mountains of Troodos. Nature trails are marked on the island, but these are not unified and many different signs are in use. At the beginning of the nature trails there is usually a map board with some information about the length and terrain and sometimes about the vegetation. Plants, flowers and trees are labelled along the trail so you can learn to

Map board

Besparmak long-distance trail sign; marker pyramid in North Cyprus;
iron arrow in South Cyprus; direction marker in South Cyprus

recognise them. Benches are placed at some of the best viewpoints.

Some of the trails described in this book are based on nature trails. The Department of Forests has a booklet of the island's nature trails (see 'Tourist information', above), but some villages have created their own trails nearby and those are not listed by the CTO (Cyprus Tourism Organisation). Some of these routes start by the roadside and might end at a picnic site or another roadside; in such cases it is necessary to arrange a pick-up or plan to retrace your steps. These routes are usually not too long and walking back on the same path you may enjoy slightly different views. Paths used by walkers but not designated as nature

trails often have occasional painted arrows and cairns.

The European Long Distance Path is marked with 'E4'. The E4 runs through Portugal, Spain, France, Switzerland, Germany, Austria, Hungary, Romania, Bulgaria, mainland Greece and Crete. The section in Cyprus was added in 2005 and it connects Paphos and Larnaca airports. It often follows tarmac roads but it aims to explore the diverse scenery of Cyprus. Some of the nature trails are part of the E4 and a few walks in this book follow some scenic sections of the E4.

The landscape of Northern Cyprus is dominated by the Kyrenia mountains. An official long-distance

29

Wild donkeys of the Karpaz Peninsula

trail, the 255km-long Besparmak Trail in Northern Cyprus, is marked with a green 'B' sign. It starts at Cape Kormakitis/Kormacit and ends at the tip of the Karpaz/Karpass Peninsula. Many of the walks described in this book follow the green B signs.

Other trails are usually marked with green and white signs. However, on some trails you can see red, blue and yellow paint marks on rocks, which are often helpful when the path is overgrown. The start points of trails are usually marked with a wooden trail gate.

There are numbered pyramids at junctions, marked on the maps found at the beginning of the trails, to help orientation. Pyramids are mentioned in the walk descriptions and marked on the maps in this book.

USING THIS GUIDE

An information box at the start of each walk provides the following information: start/finish point (including GPS coordinates), length of walk in kilometres, amount of ascent/descent in metres, difficulty rating (see grading information below), the length of time the walk is likely to take, and any details about refreshments and access that may be useful in planning. Note that where parking is mentioned it often refers to an informal parking area rather than an official car park. (At picnic sites there are usually plenty of places to park, and there are also often places for a couple of cars near the information board at the beginning of trails.)

The grading in this guide is only an indicator; bad weather, poor visibility and other factors can make any walk more challenging and even dangerous.

Grade 1: easy and/or short walk. Trail is without any significant ascent/descent. Waymarked route.

Grade 2: moderate, medium length or longer walk but mostly on easy terrain.

Grade 3: long walk and/or difficult terrain, or challenging route-finding.

The times provided – both for the walks themselves and between landmarks – are only an approximate indication. You should always allow extra time. The walk times do not take account of longer breaks for picnics or visiting a monument, castle or church.

The times and distances given in the route information boxes and route summary table are from the start to the finish of the walk. On there-and-back walks, the time is for the whole walk. On linear routes where the finish is different from the start, you will have to either arrange onward transport or retrace your steps to the start, in which case you would need to factor in additional walking time.

When planning a walk it is advisable to use Open Street Map (www.openstreetmap.org), Google Maps (www.maps.google.com) or a tourist map (available from tourist offices) to help locate the start-point. Access to the beginning of the trails is described in as much detail as possible. To help identify the exact spot, GPS coordinates are also given. These are especially useful in Northern Cyprus where the access is often difficult to describe, as roads

View of Chrysochou Bay (Walk 5)

are not numbered and the available maps don't show street names in villages. Furthermore, many trails start from or end at a remote place or outside a village.

Where there is water available on the route it is noted in the walk description, but you should never rely on it entirely as the tap or fountain might not be working at the picnic site when you get there. Occasionally there are warning signs – often only in Greek – that the water is non-potable (Μη Ποσιμο Νερο/ΜΗ ΠΟΣΙΜΟ ΝΕΡΟ). Always carry enough drinking water for your day.

Always try and check the visiting hours of churches given in this book as they can change from year to year.

In this guide, the spelling of place names in walk descriptions matches the spelling used on the maps in the guide, rather than what might be seen on signposts on the ground (which can vary along the trail). In addition, place names are given in both Greek and Turkish where both are in common use.

Places and features shown on the route maps are marked in **bold** in route descriptions to aid navigation. The term 'viewpoint' is often used to describe a place where you can get great views; this might simply be from a rock rather than a signposted viewpoint. Designated, marked viewpoints are noted as such in the route description.

SOUTHERN CYPRUS

The arc of a Venetian watermill between Sinti Monastery and Roudia Bridge (Walk 8)

THE WEST AND THE AKAMAS PENINSULA

Coastal view from Moutti tis Sotiras (Walk 1)

The westernmost and least-inhabited part of the island, the Akamas Peninsula, is home to some of the best-known walking trails on Cyprus. Part of the Akamas Peninsula was once used by the British army as a firing range, but today it is a peaceful area for wildlife and for many of Cyprus' endemic plants. The rugged coastline is washed by turquoise water and it is not difficult to see why Aphrodite and her lover Adonis might have chosen to meet in this part of the island.

The area offers a variety of walks, from the dramatic Avakas Gorge to Paphos Forest where some of the intact medieval (Venetian) bridges can be found, as well as a walk between vineyards near Panagia village.

Paphos/Baf is a great base for those who want to explore the trails in the west of the island. From self-catering accommodation to luxury hotels and resorts, tourists are spoiled for choice. For people who are fascinated by ancient history, there are plenty of ruins to discover. Paphos is known for its rich archaeological sites; the Paphos Archaeological Park, near the harbour, is famous for the mosaic floors of its Roman villas. The Tombs of the Kings – where aristocrats were buried in grand tombs carved out of rocks from around 4BC – is a UNESCO World Heritage Site.

When the walking and sightseeing are over, there are plenty of restaurants at Paphos harbour where a range of Cypriot dishes can be enjoyed.

WALK 1

Aphrodite Trail, Akamas Peninsula

Start/Finish	Bath of Aphrodite (N35.05610, E32.34589)
Distance	7.5km (4½ miles)
Ascent/Descent	500m/500m
Grade	2
Time	3hr
Refreshments	Restaurant and bar at start point
Access	Road signs are easy to follow from Paphos and Polis. Regular buses from Polis. Parking available.

This is one of the most popular and well-known nature trails on the Akamas Peninsula. Coachloads of tourists visit the Bath of Aphrodite, but not all of them follow the goddess' footsteps all the way along this scenic circular trail. It is a moderately easy walk with gentle but stony uphill sections populated by juniper trees, with a steep descent giving excellent views to the Akamas Peninsula.

During the walk you can learn to recognise some of the plants of Cyprus, as many trees and flowers are labelled. The route is signposted with iron arrows and there are benches at the best viewpoints along the way.

There is a car park and a restaurant just outside of the Botanical Garden. Go through the gate – closing it behind you as the sign requests – and then walk on the paved path which leads to the **Bath of Aphrodite**.

The **Bath of Aphrodite** is a small pool of water where a sign confirms that 'the Goddess of love and beauty used to bathe in the small pool of this natural grotto'. The pool area is usually very busy with people posing in front of the dripping water.

From the Bath, continue on the path marked 'Nature Trail'. When this paved path ends, exit through a gate then a few metres later turn left where a sign says 'Aphrodite

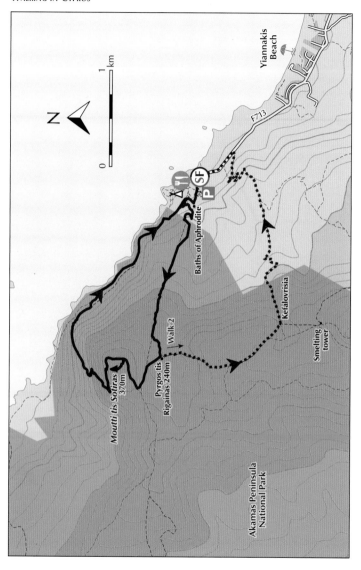

and Adonis Trail'. The two trails run together for the first 2.5km, starting from the information board. ▶

Start walking slightly uphill on a stony path with occasional glimpses of the sea. Keep on the winding, well-trodden path, ignoring a narrow path on the right

According to legend, this trail was used by Aphrodite to walk back to her tower after bathing in the pool.

APHRODITE

There are two legends that link Aphrodite's name to Cyprus; her birth and the time spent with her lover, Adonis. According to legend, the goddess of love and beauty rose from the sea near Paphos after Cronos cut off Uranus' genitals and threw them into the water. Aphrodite was married to Hephaestus but had many lovers, the most famous of which was Adonis. Myrrha – who was to be Adonis' mother – was cursed by Aphrodite to fall in love with her own father, King Cinyras of Cyprus. When Cinyras found out that he'd been tricked, the pregnant Myrrha was banished. She changed into a myrrh tree and the baby was born from that tree. Aphrodite took baby Adonis to Persephone (goddess of the underworld), but she returned when Adonis was a grown, handsome man. Aphrodite and Persephone both wanted to keep Adonis. Zeus dictated that Adonis would spend one third of the year with Aphrodite, one third of the year with Persephone and could decide for himself with whom he would spend the rest of the year. He chose to spend it with Aphrodite.

The path gives an excellent view of Chrysochou Bay

and noting the labelled trees and shrubs. As the path turns away from the sea the horizon fills with white limestones and pine-dotted hillsides.

Around the 1km mark the path levels out a bit and runs between thorny gorses. A few hundred metres later it crawls uphill again, and you find yourself walking on giant limestones before reaching a steeper section with some big stone steps. You are soon rewarded with views to the sea, and the path straightens again before climbing uphill for a short section after the 2km mark.

Ahead is the peak of Moutti tis Sotiras in the distance, but keep on the track gently turning away from the mountain. About 50min into the walk you arrive at a junction with a giant oak tree, a fountain and the ruins of **Pyrgos tis Rigainas** (Tower of the Queen). The trail divides here; the Aphrodite Trail continues to the right and the Adonis Trail to the left. Both are clearly marked.

Turn right on the Aphrodite Trail and follow the wide dirt road, occasionally marked with an 'E4', then turn right onto an iron arrow-marked path. Follow this marked path running parallel to a dirt road for a while. When you emerge at a wide dirt road, continue uphill with glimpses of the surrounding hills and sea. ◄

At the end of the dirt road the path splits. To the left is a 5min walk to **Moutti tis Sotiras'** rocky peak, where a magnificent panorama of the Akamas Peninsula can be enjoyed. Take this, soak up the views and then retrace your steps to the junction with the iron arrow and continue to the left.

Soon the narrow path runs downhill with views to the sea and with towering rocks on the left. Iron arrows occasionally indicate the clearly visible path. Zigzag steeply downhill between wild thyme and thorny bushes for about 40min, and when you reach the dirt road turn right, towards 'Aphrodite Bath'. This road also has E4 signs.

Walk for about 20min on the dirt road with views to the rugged coastline and the hillside. Soon after you spot the caravans in the campsite, turn right where the sign shows 'Aphrodite Bath' and walk back to the pool and then to the **car park**.

> Look for the ruins of the tower down below.

WALK 2

Adonis Trail, Akamas Peninsula

Start/Finish	Bath of Aphrodite (N35.05610, E32.34589)
Distance	7.5km (4½ miles)
Ascent/Descent	400m/400m
Grade	1
Time	2hr 30min
Refreshments	Restaurant and bar at start point
Access	Road signs are easy to follow from Paphos and Polis. Regular buses from Polis. Parking available.

The second best-known nature trail on the Akamas Peninsula runs along with the Aphrodite Trail for the first 2.5km – until the Pyrgos tis Rigainas.

A short section of the trail follows a forest track and then it runs on juniper and pine-covered hillsides, dotted with white limestones with remarkable views to the surrounding hills and the sea around the peninsula. During the second part of the walk you pass striking rock walls in a dry streambed, and the descent at the end gives grand views to Chrysochou Bay. Spring is probably the best time to enjoy this trail, when the hillside is carpeted with colourful wildflowers.

From the car park, go through the gate and follow the paved path to the **Bath of Aphrodite**, where a sign confirms that 'the Goddess of love and beauty used to bathe in the small pool of this natural grotto'.

A path marked 'Nature Trail' continues from the pool. Shortly the paved path ends; exit through a gate and a few metres later keep left as the 'Aphrodite and Adonis Trail' sign indicates. (For the first 2.5km the two trails runs together.) Follow the stony path uphill with occasional glimpses of the sea. Ignore a narrow path on the right and keep to the well-trodden path. Soon this bends away from the sea and the view is dominated by white limestones and pine-dotted hillsides.

The path levels out around the 1km mark, but a few hundreds metres later it crawls uphill again and you walk on giant limestones before reaching a steeper section with steps. There are some views to the sea and the path first levels out and then climbs uphill for a while after the 2km mark. Ahead in the distance is the peak of Moutti tis Sotiras, but the path bends away from it and about 50mins after starting the walk you arrive at a junction with a giant oak tree, a fountain and the ruins of **Pyrgos tis Rigainas** (Tower of the Queen). The trail splits here; the Adonis Trail continues to the left and Aphrodite Trail to the right.

ADONIS

Adonis – the god of beauty and desire – was born to Myrrha and King Cinyras of Cyprus. Aphrodite and Persephone both wanted to have him, and when Zeus announced that he could spend one third of the year with Aphrodite, the second third with Persephone and he could choose who to spend the rest of the year with, he chose Aphrodite. Adonis died after being attacked by a wild boar, believed to have been sent by one of the jealous gods. He died in Aphrodite's arms and anemones grow where his blood is said to have fallen.

Take the path on the left, marked 'Adonis Nature Trail' and 'E4'. The well-trodden path gently crawls uphill between bushes and juniper trees. About 20min later it crosses an overgrown track and shortly joins a forest track with a green arrow. A few metres later an E4 sign can be spotted, marking the direction of the Adonis trail. Follow the forest track downhill and leave it to the left where the green arrow and a battered E4 sign indicate. Approximately 1hr 20min into the walk you'll arrive at the forest junction of **Kefalovrisia**.

Turn left on the path marked 'Adonis Trail'. Walk alongside a dry streambed with rocks towering above on the left; in front, like a well-designed postcard, a green meadow stretches out with the blue sea in the background. The rough path, with a water pipe in the middle, runs steeply downhill and when it becomes smoother

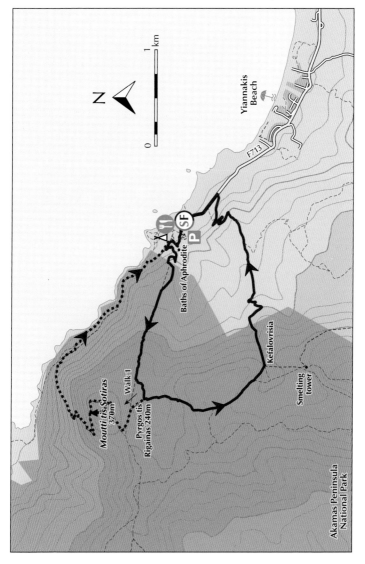

*The forest track
leading to Kefalovrisia*

you can enjoy the views without the worry of tripping over stones. Occasional green arrows and E4 signs mark the way.

The path widens and levels out, and soon the Adonis Trail leaves the wide track to the right. (There is no arrow to mark this fork, but a little green nature trail label keeps you on the right path.) You soon reach a viewpoint, from where you go steeply downhill. Ignore two consecutive dirt roads joining from the left. Shortly after the second of these, leave the track slightly to the left on the bend as the green arrow indicates. Before long there is another steep descent and you can spot the car park and restaurant near the Bath of Aphrodite, where the walk began. The path runs alongside a fence before it reaches the road; turn left on the tarmac road and walk back to the **car park**, which is 5–10min away.

WALK 3A

Smigies Nature Trail

Start/Finish	Smigies picnic site (N35.02352, E32.33367)
Distance	6.5km (4 miles)
Ascent/Descent	180m/180m
Grade	1
Time	2hr
Refreshments	None
Access	Follow the Elia Tavrou road into and through Neo Chorio village. The tarmac road turns into dirt track and leads to Smigies picnic site, where there is space to park.

Two nature trails – which could easily be tackled one after another – start from the popular Smigies picnic site. As on many nature trails, plants and flowers are labelled along the way, but the waymarks are not always consistent.

This route follows a footpath which occasionally meets and runs along a dirt road for a while. In the spring, rock roses and wildflowers colour the hillside of Pissouroumoutti. It might not be a challenging walk but remarkable views welcome you on Pissouroumoutti. Most of the walk is exposed without much shade.

Start at the Smigies picnic site by the information board showing a map of the circular walk and take the stony path that winds uphill behind the board. The landscape is dominated by Pissouroumoutti's rocky top on the left. ▶

About 15min after leaving the picnic site you arrive at a viewpoint, from where there is a clear view towards the sea. (If you observe the rugged coastline carefully,

There is no shade on the hillside and it can get very hot on a sunny day.

43

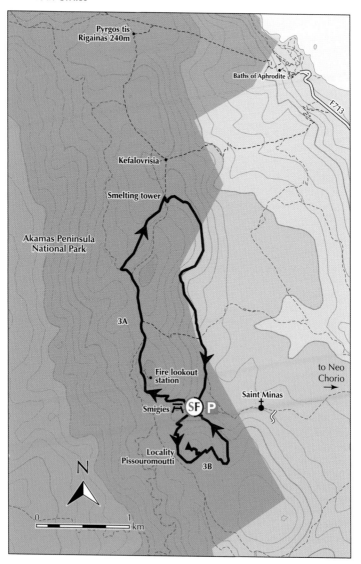

Pyrgos tis Rigainas 240m

Baths of Aphrodite

F713

Kefalovrisia

Smelting tower

Akamas Peninsula National Park

3A

to Neo Chorio

Fire lookout station

Saint Minas

Smigies

P

Locality Pissouromoutti

3B

N

0   1

km

you may spot some sea coves.) On the right at the top of the rocky hill is the Piana fire lookout station building. Continue on the path and soon reach a dirt road; keep left, as the green arrow indicates, and follow this slightly downhill (the right fork goes up to the **fire lookout station**).

Continue on the track – lined with pines and with sea views on the left – to the next intersection, where you follow the nature trail sign straight on. Soon you arrive at another intersection, where the path on the right-hand side is the short version of the nature trail and returns to Smigies picnic site. Follow the 'Long Way 5km' sign on

Smelting tower by the former magnesium mine

45

the wider track, straight on. Here the path runs on level ground with excellent views. Ignore the adjoining dirt road on the right and keep straight on as the track bends slightly left. Very soon, at the next junction, go right as the green arrow indicates.

Follow the dirt track slightly downhill by the dry streambed. ◀ Pass the ruins of a house and then go downhill. After the 3km mark, follow the green arrow to the left. Approximately an hour after leaving Smigies picnic site, notice the **smelting tower** of a former magnesium mine on your right. Walk up to the tower and a little further on you will find the shafts of the mine.

Juniper and pine trees are the main vegetation on both sides of the road.

A number of **magnesium mines** in the Akamas region were abandoned at beginning of the 20th century. Today the remains of kilns indicate the former mining activity.

Standing with the kiln and entrance holes on your right, continue straight on and slightly downhill, on a narrow path between bushes. Soon spot the green arrow sign. The stony path runs along the rock rose-covered hillside with views to Chrysochou Bay. The fire lookout station comes back into view and you descend gently. Keep on the small path, ignoring other paths crossing your way. This becomes smoother and runs beneath pine trees before descending on the rocky hillside.

When the path meets a dirt road, keep straight on. (The small path joining in from the right is the other end of the 'short way' that peeled off from the nature trail after the fire lookout station.) When the dirt road splits, follow the one on the right and walk back to the **Smigies picnic site**.

WALK 3B

Pissouromoutti Nature Trail

Start/Finish	Smigies picnic site (N35.02352, E32.33367)
Distance	3km (1¾ miles)
Ascent/Descent	175m/175m
Grade	1
Time	1hr 15min
Refreshments	None
Access	Follow the Elia Tavrou road into and through Neo Chorio village. The tarmac road turns into dirt track and leads to Smigies picnic site.

At the opposite end of the Smigies picnic site there is another information board with a map of the short Pissouromoutti Trail. The circular route starts gently uphill just behind this board.

From the Pissouromoutti information board, start on the path winding gently uphill on the right. The path follows the contour of the hillside and just after the 0.5km mark it bends away from the fire lookout station, with excellent views to the sea on the right.

For map see Walk 3A

Locality Pissouromoutti

About 30min later you'll reach a junction with a 'Pissouromoutti View Point' sign. From here it is possible to follow the narrow, grassy path running amid rocks and overgrown by wildflowers, to the top. The path might be difficult to spot. On the peak of Pissouromoutti (**Locality Pissouromoutti**) (400m) a fantastic 360-degree panorama greets you.

From the peak, retrace your steps to the junction with the viewpoint sign and continue downhill to the left. This section is easy to follow as it descends gently on a grassy path. A few minutes later, join a track overgrown by grass; keep right and follow it for about 50m.

Leave the track to the left on a narrow path, marked with a good-sized arrow made of stones on the grass. This pleasant path descends through lush vegetation to a forest road, which is only 5–10min away from the stone arrow. Turn left onto this and a few metres later take the path on the left. It first runs parallel to the forest road, then gradually leaves it behind and returns to **Smigies picnic site**.

WALK 4
Avakas Gorge

Start/Finish	Car park 900m E of Toxeftra Beach (N34.92048, E32.33796)
Distance	11.5km (7 miles); return via gorge: 10.5km (6½ miles)
Ascent/Descent	440m/440m; return via gorge: 320m/320m
Grade	3
Time	4hr 30min–5hr; return via gorge: 6hr
Refreshments	Viklari restaurant near the gorge; restaurants at Agios Georgios and Lara Beach; water at car park
Access	From Agios Georgios on F706 road, head north towards Lara, follow to Viklary 'The Last Castle' car park and turn right towards Avakas Gorge. It is a dirt road but in fairly good condition; in dry weather most cars can take it without any problem.

The first half of this walk involves a scramble through huge, impressive rocks in a narrow gorge. Following the Avgas river, you hop from rock to rock in the water surrounded by massive rock walls. Most people only walk up to the narrowest part of the gorge, so the further you get the fewer people you are likely to encounter. At the end of the gorge you can either retrace your steps or return to the car park via a dirt track.

As the gorge is very narrow near its start, the water level can rise rapidly after heavy rain and create a flash flood. It might not be possible to pass the narrow section if the water level is high. During heavy rain or thunderstorms walkers should avoid the gorge.

In addition, rocks can be slippery and the ground is loose in many places. There is a risk of rockfall and grazing goats could knock down rocks from above at any time.

About 900m from Toxeftra Beach there is a designated car park with a picnic area, information board and toilets. The stony path starts by the information board and immediately crosses the stream. It then runs between juniper trees for 8–10min before arriving at another information board.

About 800m from the car park you enter the gorge. There is a towering limestone wall on your right as you walk on the narrow but well-trodden path by the stream. Cross the stream on rocks several times before reaching the narrowest part of the gorge.

The **Avakas Gorge** was formed by and named after the Avgas river. The name Avgas originates from the Greek word for egg, and it refers to the fact that many birds – including the endemic Cyprus wheatear and Cyprus warbler – live and nest in the gorge.

Water has eroded the limestone rocks, creating an impressive narrow gorge.

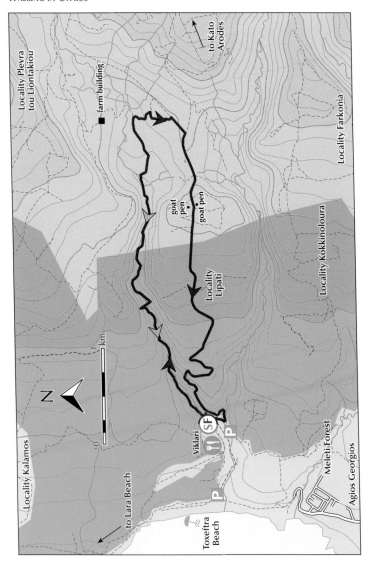

Locality Plevra
tou Liontakiou

to Kato
Arodes

farm building

Locality Farkonia

goat
pen

goat pen

Locality
Lipati

Locality Kokkinoloura

N

1 km

0

Locality Kalamos

Viklari

SF

P

P

Meleti Forest

Agios Georgios

to Lara Beach

Toxeftra
Beach

*One of the many
river crossings
along the trail*

▸ Look up to see the huge rock stuck between the edges of the gorge above you. From here, you scramble and climb through many boulders of various sizes and cross the stream numerous times before reaching the end of the gorge.

Soon after its narrowest section the gorge widens up a bit, with bushes and trees clinging to the rock walls and the banks of the stream becoming denser. About 3km into the gorge there is a rockfall on the right, and shortly after that another one on the left. It might be difficult to see the path here, but stay close to the stream. Ignore the small

Enormous rocks cast shade into the thin pass; birds swoop and settle on their nests built into the sheer rock face.

Most people only walk up to the narrowest section of the gorge

(goat) path leading up to the right and stay by the stream, which you cross several times on rocks as you progress.

The ground might be loose here, so extra care should be taken. You may have to deviate from the 'main' path depending on the water level and vegetation on the banks as well as rockfalls.

Just before 4km, notice a big plane tree with its roots clinging to the loose soil on the left. Climb up to the ledge and arrive at a clearing with wildflowers and with limestone cliffs on the left. A few minutes later you are back to the streambed; continue between boulders and rocks.

At nearly 5km you'll see a rusty old trailer crushed on rocks to the left-hand side. A few minutes later you'll spot the other part of the trailer in the water, partially buried under the sediment. Soon another riverbed joins from the right, but carry straight on to reach a narrow section overgrown with reeds. There is a 'path' on the ledge on loose, scrambling chalky rock, but it is safer to go through the reeds. Shortly afterwards, climb out of the gorge onto a grassy clearing.

> The nearby green and white **hills** are dotted with goats and sheep. Grassy lands scattered with white chalk and limestone patches dominate the surrounding hills.

There are two options here: you can either return the way you came or take a circular route back to the start.

Return via the gorge
If you enjoyed scrambling through boulders in the gorge you might want go back the same way – but allow at least the same amount of time for returning as it took to reach this point.

If you want to get back to the car park a bit quicker, or if it is not safe to return through the gorge due to rain or the threat of rain, there is an option to walk back on a dirt track. It might not be easy to find, but once you find it, it takes about an hour (5.5km) to get back to the car park.

As you emerge from the gorge to the grassy clearing, turn right (south). There is a stone cairn; walk towards it and carry on uphill for about 50m, where you will find two isolated shrubs close to each other. Just after the shrubs a faint path can be seen in the grass on the left. Go left on this overgrown path and when you reach a track mark on the grass, follow it between old olive trees.

At an intersection keep right (the left-hand option goes downhill towards a farm). Shortly afterwards, go slightly left uphill and at the next 'junction' (faint) keep right. There is a network of track marks on the grass, but you need to head south-south-east. A white chalky track becomes visible well before you reach it; on reaching it go right, and at a junction right again. Continue on here all the way back to the car park.

About 30min after reaching the white chalky track you pass some ramshackle **goat pens** with sheep and goats nearby. As you descend between juniper trees, enjoy spectacular views to the shore, Lara Beach and then Agios Georgios by the sea. Ignore a track on the left and shortly arrive back at the **car park**.

WALK 5
Argaka Nature Trail

Start/Finish	South east corner of Argaka village (N35.05957, E32.49749)
Distance	10.5km (6½ miles)
Ascent/Descent	300m/300m
Grade	1
Time	2hr 40min
Refreshments	None en route
Access	From Polis take the E704 road (Mariou Road) to Argaka village. Turn right onto Makarios III Avenue and after the primary school at the junction carry straight on. When the road splits, stay on the left fork and this will take you to the information board that marks the beginning of the trail. There is space to park near the information board.

This walk follows snaking dirt tracks with scenic views to the hills and coast. A network of tracks criss-crosses the hillside but the nature trail is well marked. Pine trees proudly line the way but on sunny days the route is exposed to the sun without much shade. Rock roses, thatching grass, olives and prickly burnet grow wild by the route.

Start uphill on the tarmac road with the information board on your right, and a few metres later the road becomes a dirt track. ◀ Just a few minutes after the start, pass a water tank; ignore the track joining in from the left. After the 1km mark the track bends to the left with views to pine-covered hills. When the track splits, follow the left-hand fork. (You will return to this junction towards the end of the walk.)

Immediately there are views to Chrysochou Bay on the right and Argaka on the left.

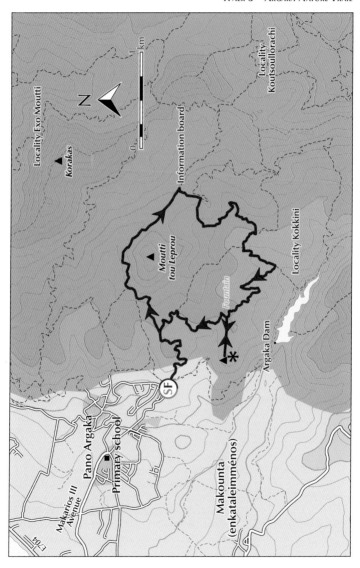

55

The Argaka Trail follows forest tracks

As you continue slightly uphill, notice some narrow-leaved cistus and Calabrian pines by the track. To the left there are splendid views to Chrysochou Bay and the houses of Argaka can also be spotted.

Ignore any tracks joining in from the left before the 2km sign. For the next kilometre the track undulates gently alongside pine trees, and after the 3km mark you walk on the ridge with views on both sides: Paphos Forest on the left, and Chrysochou Bay and Akamas on the right.

About 1hr into the walk, arrive at an **information board** and take the track on the right. Soon look out for a plant label indicating that you are on the nature trail. A few minutes later, turn right to a track going downhill. ▸ After the 4km mark the track runs steeply downhill and bends left beneath pines as it follows the contour of the valley.

Once again you have views to the bay.

At the next junction go right, steeply downhill, and soon cross the riverbed of Argaki tou Kampiou. Continue on the track with a shallow valley on the left. At the next intersection keep right, going slightly uphill as the 'Nature Trail Short Way 4km' sign indicates. The track turns away from the valley; on the left there is another small, dry streambed which you cross as the track bends again. There are splendid views to mountains on the left as you gently ascend.

About 20min after taking the 'short way' track you come to a bench with a **fountain**. ▸ From here you can make a worthwhile 450m detour to a **viewpoint**.

Unfortunately the water is not drinkable!

> **Argaka Dam** can be seen from here. It was built in 1964 and supplies water for irrigation of agricultural crops in the Argaka area.

Return to the bench and fountain and continue onwards. You pass a series of stone pines by the track as it steadily goes downhill. About 20min after the fountain, arrive at the junction where the track split at the beginning of the walk. Go left and walk back to the information board.

WALK 6
Horteri Nature Trail

Start/Finish	Locality Platanouthkia, east of Stavros tis Psokas (N35.02503, E32.63483)
Distance	5km (3 miles)
Ascent/Descent	460m/460m
Grade	1
Time	1hr 30min–2hr
Refreshments	The nearest is in Stavros tis Psokas
Access	Locality Platanouthkia is about 2km east from Stavros tis Psokas on the F723 road. The drive to the start of the trail involves countless hairpin bends on a quiet and dramatic road. Parking available on roadside.

A short, peaceful and spectacular nature trail in the shade of trees with impressive views of endless forest-covered hills. The first half of the trail – on part of the E4 – climbs steadily uphill, and then the route descends on a narrow footpath.

Paphos Forest is home to over 600 different plant species. The Cyprus cedar can only be found here, and it is especially typical around Trypilos Mountain. There is a mouflon enclosure at Stavros tis Psokas, located only 2km from the beginning of the trail, providing an opportunity to see these endemic animals.

As you ascend between golden oaks and moss-covered rocks, it is possible to spot the roof of the houses of the forest station and a helipad in the distance.

Walk up the stone steps behind the roadside fountain. The path runs uphill for a few minutes and then splits; go sharply left, uphill as the E4 sign indicates. You will arrive back at this junction at end of the walk.

Climb steeply uphill on the narrow, stony path beneath trees and then zigzag on the hillside with views to the forest-covered mountains. ◄ About 15min after

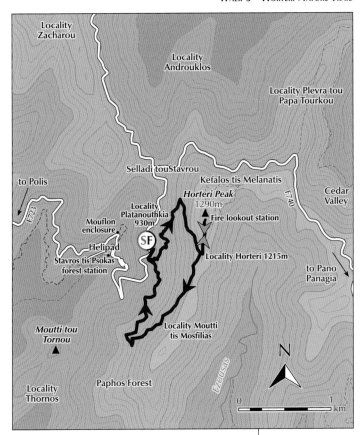

turning left at the intersection you arrive at the first of several benches designated as special viewpoints, from where the Stavros river valley near the forest station and the Zacharon fire lookout station on a distant hilltop can be seen on a clear day. Soon the path takes a sharp U-turn to the right and continues uphill with mountain views now on the right. About 1hr into the walk you reach the **Locality Horteri** sign at 1215m.

Bird's-eye view of Stavros tis Psokas in Paphos Forest

The main trail continues downhill beneath trees, slightly to the right, but first there is an option to climb to the top of Horteri. The ascent path is not clearly marked and the summit, with a huge antenna, fire look-out platform and the ruins of a building, might be a bit disappointing – but the views are great. Allow 25min return.

Ascent of Horteri

From Locality Horteri, take the wider path marked 'E4', slightly uphill on the left. Follow the wide path for 5–7min and as the track bends to the right the antenna on top of Horteri comes into sight. It is a long way on the forest track to get to the top, so you might consider a short-cut here: just when the forest track bends right, slightly downhill, there is a clearing on the left-hand side, and if you carefully observe the bushes you will see a stone cairn. An overgrown but distinguishable path leads straight to the top. From here it takes 5–6min to get to the summit between shrubs.

From the **summit** there are scenic views towards the Cedar Valley, Troodos mountains and Chrysochou Bay;

admire the panorama and then retrace your steps back to the Locality Horteri sign and the junction with the bench.

To continue on the main trail, go slightly downhill: coming from Horteri's summit it is the path on the left; if you didn't go to the top it is the path on the right. The very narrow path runs along the hillside with views now on the right. ▶ About 40min into the descent, the path makes a sudden U-turn to the right and soon the road comes into view. Reach the junction with the E4 sign where you took the other branch earlier. Go downhill and a few minutes later arrive back at **Locality Platanouthkia**.

Moss-covered trees often obstruct the views but there are plenty of viewpoints along the descent.

WALK 7
Vouni path

Start/Finish	Pano Panagia (N34.91832, E32.63142)
Distance	8.5km (5¼ miles); via the monastery: 10.5km (6½ miles)
Ascent/Descent	340m/340m; via the monastery: 460m/460m
Grade	2
Time	3hr; via the monastery: 3hr 40min (+ allow extra time to visit the monastery)
Refreshments	Pano Panagia
Access	Pano Panagia is located on the E606 road, which can be accessed from the B6. There are daily buses from Paphos.

This route follows meandering, occasionally steep dirt roads through well-maintained old vineyards. The track meets several other tracks wriggling between the cultivated land, but the Vouni path is easy to follow and there are signs at every junction. Excellent panoramas can be enjoyed throughout this trail and visiting the Chrysorrogiatissa Monastery with its relaxing atmosphere can complete the day perfectly. The monks make their own wine; don't miss the opportunity to buy a bottle.

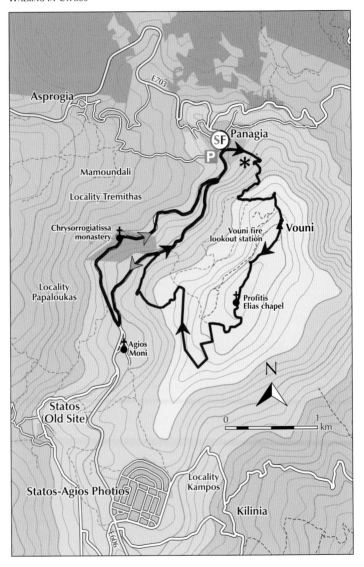

The trail starts by the information board in Pano Panagia.

> **Pano Panagia** is the birthplace of Archbishop Makarios III (1913–1977), the first president of the Republic of Cyprus from 1960 until his death in 1977.

Start on the tarmac road (Agiou Georgiou) that runs steeply uphill by a vineyard. The Vouni path is clearly signposted and as with most nature trails, many plants are labelled along the way. After ascending for about 10min, at an intersection take the wide, stony track on the right. Soon there are views to Pano Panagia village and a few minutes later there is an opportunity to admire the panorama from a **viewpoint** located on the right, clearly visible from the road bend.

> From the roofed **viewing platform** you can spot the Triplos and Moutti tous Anemous mountain peaks, among many others, as well as Kannaviou Dam in the distance, while listening to the echoes from Panagia.

From the viewpoint retrace your steps to the road bend and continue uphill between terraced vineyards. Tracks adjoin the stony trail but there are signs indicating the right direction. Reach an information board about the unique Cyprus vegetation about 20min after the viewpoint; from here the track climbs vigorously uphill and then runs between vineyards again. There are fine views to the mountains of Troodos before you pass a **fire lookout station** at 1135m, about 20min after the information board.

Just after the fire lookout building the track levels out a bit. Continue between vineyards and then shortly reach the second viewpoint, from where you can spot Chrysorrogiatissa Monastery. Continue on the track and soon arrive at **Profitis Elias chapel**, from where you start to descend.

At the first junction after the church go right, and at the next intersection bear left. There are some rocks and bushes around the dirt track but soon – once again – the scenery is dominated by vineyards.

Keep right at the next two junctions. The track swings steadily downhill with views to cultivated slopes with mountains in the background and you can even spot Agios Moni down on the left. At the intersection before a water tank, go right as an arrow indicates. Soon, as you descend steeply, the houses of Pano Panagia come into view.

To visit Chrysorrogiatissa Monastery
To visit the monastery, turn left at the junction with a sign to Panagia and Chrysorrogiatissa Monastery. It is 1km on

Chrysorrogiatissa Monastery

a tarmac road to reach the main road, where you turn right and walk a further 1km to reach the **monastery**. From there it is another 1.5km on the tarmac road back to **Panagia** village.

> The **Chrysorrogiatissa Monastery** was founded in 1152. Monk Ignatios found an icon of the Virgin Mary near Paphos, and built a monastery in the mountains, dedicated to 'Our Lady of the Golden Pomegranate'. The present building – home to a collection of icons – dates back to 1770. The monastery's old winery makes some fine wines from grapes grown in its vineyards.

Alternatively, rather than following the sign to Chrysorrogiatissa Monastery, you can walk straight back to **Panagia** (1.5km) on the tarmac road on the right.

WALK 8
Sinti Monastery – Roudia Bridge

Start/Finish	Sinti Monastery (N34.83687, E32.64141)
Distance	17km (10½ miles)
Ascent/Descent	290m/290m
Grade	2
Time	4hr 30min–5hr
Refreshments	None: take plenty of drinking water
Access	Leave the E606 road for Old Pentalia village and follow the narrow, mainly concrete road to the Sinti Monastery. Parking available at start point.

This there-and-back route follows a wide, stony track in the Xeros river valley, with several exciting river crossings and ruins of watermills to admire along the way. It starts and finishes at the Panagia tou Sinti Monastery, which stands peacefully on the west bank of the Xeros. For a very short section, the far leg of the walk joins the Venetian Bridge Nature Trail (see Walk 9).

NOTE

Although this is an easy walk, be prepared to cross the Xeros river bare-foot (or wear hiking sandals). The water can be really cold and fast-flowing in places. Rocks are slippery, therefore extra care needs to be taken when crossing. If the water level is high, crossing might not be possible or can be very dangerous.

In the valley, walkers can be exposed to strong sun without any shade: it is advisable to take a hat.

Park by the Panagia tou Sinti Monastery, from where the route starts.

> Dedicated to the Virgin Mary, the Orthodox Monastery of **Panagia tou Sinti** was founded in the 16th century. It was used until 1927 and then in the early 1950s its property was sold to the nearby villages. The abandoned building deteriorated rapidly and restoration work only started in 1993. The monastery received a Europa Nostra Award for preserving the original character of the building and it is under UNESCO protection.

The rocks can be slippery, especially underwater, and water flow can be fast in places, so extra care needs to be taken when crossing.

Walk down to the riverbank. The stony dirt road continues on the other side of the Xeros river. This is the first of the many river crossings you encounter along the way. Depending on how deep and fast the river is at the time of your visit, you might be able to find rocks to hop on, in order to cross. You may need to walk up or downstream a bit to find the best crossing point, but if you want to save time you could just cross the river barefoot. ◄

In spring, wildflowers colour this wide valley that is surrounded by green hills.

The dirt road runs through the valley parallel to the river with a vineyard on your right. Some 20–25min after leaving the monastery, arrive at a simple, **concrete bridge**. Go over it and take the dirt road on the right. Almost immediately after the bridge, cross another branch of the river and then pass an **orange grove** on your left. Keep on the track, and at a junction go right on the dirt road running closer to the river. ◄

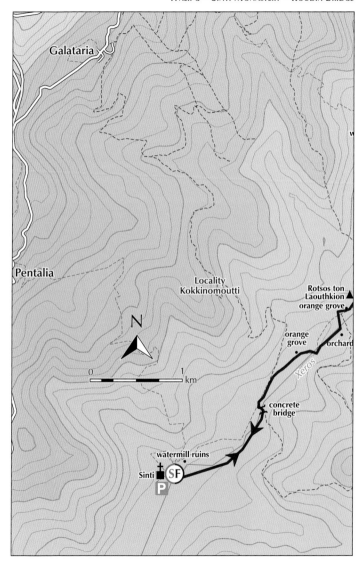

Very soon, cross the river twice in quick succession and continue on the track with the river on your left and the rocky hill, Rotsos ton Laouthkion, in front of you. After passing a fenced area on the right, cross the river again and then walk by an untidy **orchard**.

Soon after the orchard the river is hidden from view by trees, but the sound of rushing water signals its existence. Cross a small stream joining the Xeros close to **Rotsos ton Laouthkion**. After the crossing, on your left spot an overgrown rock with red and blue arrows painted on it. The blue arrow points towards the dirt track, but the red one points towards the trees, where in the shade there is a charming place to stop for a rest by the river.

A charming spot in the shade of trees near Rotsos ton Laouthkion

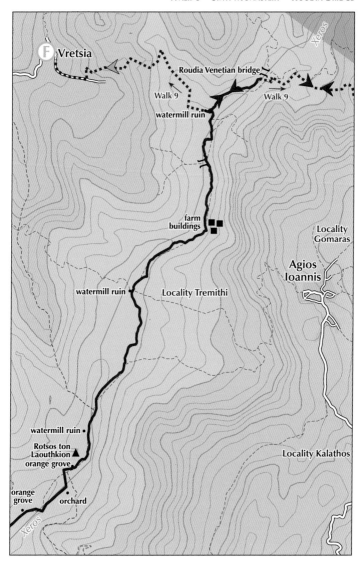

Remains of a Venetian watermill

It might be slightly deeper here (most probably you will have to take your boots off).

Continue on the track as the blue arrow indicates and soon see the ruins of a **watermill** on the left. Less then 10min after the ruins, cross the river again. ◄ Continue on the track, which bends away from the Xeros somewhat, and ignore the dirt road – which goes to Agios Ioannis – on the right.

The road winds through the valley dotted with olive trees and shrubs and with splendid views of the distant hills. About 15min after crossing the river there is another ruin of a **watermill** on the left. Note the huge rock with faded red and blue arrows on it. With the ruins on your left, continue straight on along the dirt track as the red arrow suggests. Ignore a track joining from your left, pass by a **farm** and keep on the dirt track. Ignore a bridge, carry straight on and soon, where the track splits, keep left.

About 20min after the farm, cross the river for the last time. Walk towards the ruins of another **watermill** in front of you. The Venetian Bridge Nature Trail (Walk 9) runs just above the ruins on the hillside; climb up to the path on the grassy area on the left side of the ruins. Turn right on the path, which first runs parallel to a dirt road and a plantation, and then about 15min later arrives at **Roudia Bridge**.

Roudia Bridge is one of the stone bridges built in the mountains as part of a 'camel trail' during Cyprus' Venetian period (1489–1671). Good-quality routes were essential for the transportation of copper by camel from the mountains to the ports.

From Roudia Bridge, retrace your steps to the monastery. Alternatively you can continue to Vretsia, as described in Walk 9, and organise transport from there.

WALK 9
Venetian bridges

Start/Finish	Kelefos Bridge (N34.88948, E32.74748)
Alternative Finish	Vretsia village
Distance	16km (10 miles); alternative finish: 11km (6¾ miles)
Ascent/Descent	750m/750m; alternative finish: 560m/440m
Grade	3
Time	5hr 30min; alternative finish: 3hr 45min
Refreshments	None
Access	From F616 road near Agios Nikolaos, take the E810. This narrow asphalt road takes you to Kelefos Bridge. There are plenty of places to park near the bridge.

The out-and-back walk described here is part of the 17km-long nature trail connecting Kaminaria and Vretsia villages via Venetian bridges. From Kelefos Bridge the often narrow and steep path winds along hillsides with fantastic views to mountains, criss-crossing forest tracks before reaching Roudia Bridge. Roudia Bridge is hidden in the forest and only seen by those who either walk there on forest tracks or drive in 4x4 vehicles. The route is marked as a nature trail but it is far from the other well-known and busy nature trails on the island. The forest is serene; dirt tracks, a few plantations and ruins are the only reminders of human activity in the area.

From Roudia Bridge you can continue to abandoned Vretsia village, but you will have to organise a pick-up/transport from there.

Kelefos Bridge was built by the Venetians

Walk down to and cross Kelefos Bridge. At the foot of the bridge there is an information board about the Venetian Bridges Nature Trail, with a map and distance information.

> Stone **bridges** were built in the mountains as part of a 'camel trail' during Cyprus' Venetian period (1489–1671). Good-quality routes were essential to transport copper by camel from the mountains to the ports.

This type of sign is used to mark the route along the way.

A brown wooden arrow with a yellow tip points to a path just behind the information board. ◀ The narrow, stony path zigzags steeply uphill through the pine forest for about 10min then reaches a forest track. Turn right and 200m later, at a junction, go left.

About 5min later, in a clearing, continue straight on. Soon – when the track joins another forest road – carry straight on again. Ignore a track on the left and then keep right when you see the next sign. Walk slightly downhill in pine forest, with the sound of trickling water from the ravine on the right. When the track is crossed by another

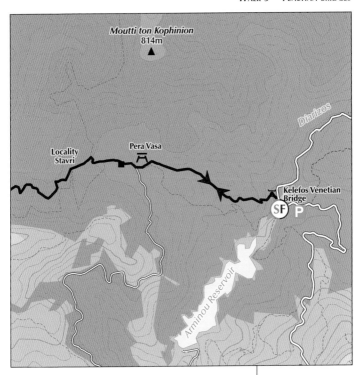

dirt road, continue straight on as the yellow arrow indicates.

About 30min (2km) after leaving Kelefos Bridge, arrive at **Pera Vasa picnic site**. Go around the picnic area and pass the huge trunk of a 200-year-old Calabrian pine. Continue to the right, with ruins of a building on the left. By the remains of the wall, go towards Mylikouri. Pass a house on the left and ignore the track on the left at the end of the property. A yellow arrow indicates the direction when the track forks to the left (a dirt road on the right goes towards Agios Ioannis).

About 30–40min after leaving Pera Vasa, arrive at **Locality Stavri**. Continue downhill on a narrow footpath, which starts near the 'Locality Stavri' sign, as the familiar yellow arrow indicates. Follow the undulating path for about 15–20min, first beneath trees and then with views to the pine-covered mountains.

When you emerge onto a wide dirt track, turn right. The track bends left with magnificent mountain views on the right. A couple of minutes later, cross two forest tracks very close to each other. Both times, an arrow indicates the direction. Take a few steps up to the 'Spilios tou Saouri' sign and keep right by a fence. About 10min later, keep on the path on the left, leaving the dirt road and the fenced plantation.

You soon cross a wide chalk track, and once again the stony path runs along a hillside with impressive views, then descends steeply. ◄ Shortly after the **Mantra tou Mita** sign the rough path comes very close to a dirt road but veers left away from it, and you start a very steep descent. Then climb gently to a clearing and continue on its other side; stone cairns might be there to help.

From the left, like a curious face, a pale white cliff with thick green vegetation on its top stares down to a deep, narrow valley.

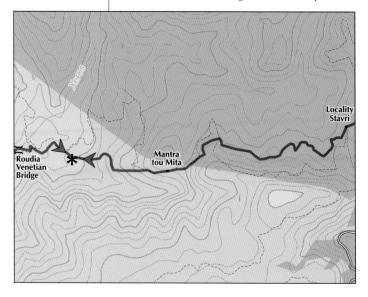

74

Descending on the narrow path towards Roudia Bridge

After another descent, arrive at a forest track with a two-sided arrow. Go left downhill, and soon reach a **viewpoint** with two benches. Shortly after that, when you reach another track with a two-way arrow, bear left downhill. At this point you can hear the sound of rushing water; follow the signs and you will soon arrive at the grand **Roudia Bridge**.

From here you have two options: retrace your steps to Kelefos Bridge, or continue for 3km to the abandoned Vretsia village.

To Vretsia village

Cross Roudia Bridge and continue on its other side. The narrow, sometimes loose-surfaced path runs along an eroded rock wall. It runs parallel to a dirt road and a plantation on the left. Some 15–20min after leaving Roudia Bridge, pass the ruins of a **watermill**. (Walk 8 shares the section between the watermill ruins and Roudia Bridge.) The path might be overgrown here but it continues along the hillside and soon crosses a small stream by a huge rock before joining a dirt road. Keep right and soon there are two junctions close together; both times, keep right,

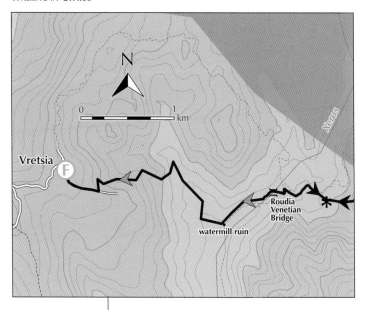

The path is
occasionally exposed
and the surface loose.

close to the stream. Stay on the narrow footpath and
ignore the track on the left. ◀

The path runs uphill and after a meadow it turns
away from the stream. For 35–45min walk mainly uphill,
sometimes steeply. When the path crosses a forest track,
continue on its other side. Walk through pine forest with
occasional views to the mountains.

Emerging onto a dirt road, turn right and walk to
Vretsia village.

> **Vretsia** was a Turkish Cypriot village and was aban-
> doned as a result of the 1974 conflict. Apart from
> a house that operates as a small bar, the buildings
> have been left to slowly decay. You can wander
> among the abandoned buildings.

THE TROODOS AND CENTRAL CYPRUS

Small water reservoir near Lagoudera encircled by mountains (Walk 22)

Troodos is cooler than the coast and many of its trails can be enjoyed at most times of the year. In the winter, snow can cover the highest parts of the Troodos and its ski slopes are visited by winter sports enthusiasts.

Troodos Square is usually bustling with tourists but you can start some spectacular trails from there – and after your walk you can buy local products in the souvenir shops and have a meal in one of the restaurants. For those who want to learn more about Troodos, the Troodos Visitor Centre, located just outside of Troodos Square, is worth a visit. The village of Pano Platres – about 8km from Troodos Square – has some hotels and restaurants, and can be a great base

for people who want to explore the trails in the area.

Winding roads connect the quiet villages where Byzantine monasteries and small churches are hidden on the pine-covered slopes. A section of the long-distance E4 trail connects two UNESCO-listed churches, and you can find some charming trails near the grand Machairas Monastery. Many of the region's trails give an opportunity to visit a church or monastery or a charismatic village.

Kakopetria on the banks of the Karkotis river – where Cypriots from Nicosia/Lefkoşa own holiday homes to escape the summer heat – is another peaceful base for walkers.

WALK 10

Xystarouda – Agiasma – Vasiliki Nature Trail

Start/Finish	Xystarouda picnic site (N34.97940, E32.77986)
Distance	12km (7½ miles)
Ascent/Descent	760m/760m
Grade	2
Time	5hr–5hr 20min
Refreshments	Water at picnic site
Access	Xystarouda picnic site is on the E912 road approximately halfway between Gerakies village and Kykkos Monastery. There are places to park at the picnic site.

This there-and-back route follows an undulating path in a peaceful forest where you may spot mouflon hopping nimbly on rocks. After descending to a valley where a small stream is hidden by trees, it climbs steeply uphill with splendid views to the mountains. At the end of the trail you arrive at the small St Vasilios church encircled by mountains. As on many nature trails, you will most probably have to retrace your steps back to the picnic site.

MOUFLON

The Cyprus mouflon – a shy, light brown wild sheep – is the largest mammal in Cyprus. The male is slightly bigger than the female and can be recognised by its heavy, sickle-shaped horns. During the summer months the mouflon skilfully hop on the steep slopes of Paphos Forest in search of food. However, in the winter when the mountains might be covered with snow they live at a lower altitude.

Roman mosaics provide evidence that mouflon were around in Roman times. Aristocrats hunted them during the Middle Ages, and when the use of guns for hunting became widespread, their numbers decreased significantly.

Today, Paphos Forest is a Special Protected Area and thanks to the great effort to protect the mouflon and their habitat, their numbers have returned to a satisfactory level.

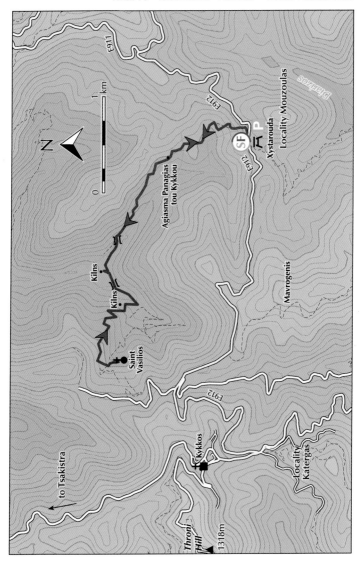

The path starts downhill close to an information board on the right-hand side of the Prodramos–Kykkos road. There are steps leading steeply downhill between golden oaks and soon some views to the mountains on the left. You might spot some faint paths, but the well-trodden nature trail is clear and easy to follow. Pine trees and golden oaks are the main vegetation as the path swings around the mountainside, heading constantly downhill for 45–50min to arrive at **Agiasma Panagias tou Kykkou** (spring). ◄

The spring is a small pool in the rock at the foot of the rock wall.

Agiasma means 'holy water'. The **spring** is believed to have appeared miraculously from the rocks and many people visit the site. Small pieces of cloth hang from a nearby tree and there are images on the wall indicating that for many this is a special place.

Continue downhill on intermittent steps with great views to the mountains, and about 10min after the spring, note an ancient olive tree on your left-hand side. As you descend, you'll soon hear the gurgling water from

A small wooden bridge connects the banks of the rushing stream

the valley on your left. Lush vegetation indicates the pres-
ence of the water and about 25–30min after the spring
you arrive at a small rushing stream.

Cross the wooden **bridge** and the fern-enveloped
path continues by the waterway. Soon start ascending,
with views to the gorge and the rocky mountain slope on
its opposite side. As the path bends away from the valley
through which the stream flows, it runs beneath very tall
pine trees. About 15min after the bridge, the path splits;
the right branch takes you to a **kiln** approximately 60m
away and the other branch is the main trail.

Continue along the mountainside and shortly you
will hear the sound of the gurgling water again. After
a short descent, arrive at a second **bridge**. The path is
only close to the stream for a few metres before it crawls
steeply uphill. Walk along the hillside with the gorge on
the left and soon climb steeply uphill again.

About 30–40min after the second bridge, pass some
old **kilns** and then continue uphill. Soon, as you're
ascending, you will spot Mt Olympus in the Troodos
in the distance on your left and some olive plantations
down in the valley. When the path starts to descend,
note some houses and the old Saint Vasilios church in the
valley. Continue downhill and arrive at an information
board at a road. To visit the **church** (open 8am–12midday
and 3.30pm–5pm), turn left and walk about 300m along
the road.

After visiting the church, retrace your steps back to
Xystarouda picnic site.

WALK 11

Prodromos Dam – Stavroulia Trail

Start/Finish	Prodromos Dam picnic site (N34.94755, E32.84712)
Distance	9.5km (6 miles)
Ascent/Descent	420m/420m
Grade	1
Time	3hr
Refreshments	None on route; restaurant in Prodromos
Access	Prodromos Dam picnic site is located on the Troodos–Prodromos (F952) road, 2.5km from Prodromos village. Parking space available.

This walk combines the best of the Prodromos – Zoumi and Prodromou – Stavroulia nature trails. It is made circular by walking on the asphalt road for about 3.5km at the end of the walk. There are viewpoints along the way where you can take time to enjoy the stunning views towards Morfou Bay, the mountains and Kykkos Monastery. Detailed nature trail labels help to identify many of the plants on this trail.

Prodromos' (1380m) cooler climate in the summer and the closeness of the ski resorts on Mt Olympus have been attracted visitors for many years. The once-luxurious Berengaria Hotel, formerly frequented by royalty, lies near the village. It opened in 1931 but was abandoned in 1984. According to local legend it is haunted by ghosts. Plans were made for restoration, however the grand building is still slowly decaying.

From the picnic site, the trail starts beneath black pine trees by the information board on the right-hand side of the road from the direction of Troodos. Walk downhill on the stony path, which soon levels out and runs on the

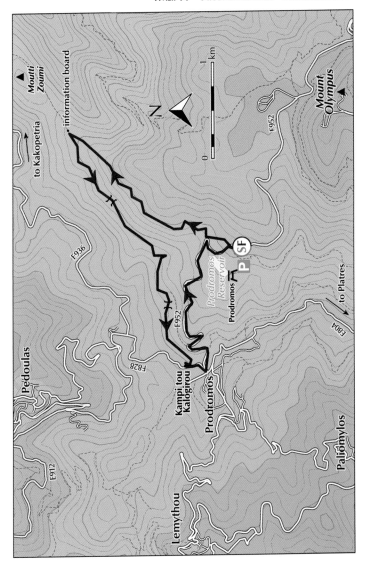

hillside between prickly junipers and Cyprus cedars. The path soon heads along a railing with views towards Pedoulas village with a Balkan war memorial on the slope encircled by mountains. ◄

Start to descend with excellent views towards Morfou Bay about 40–45min from the start of the walk. Soon spot a path to the right going to a viewpoint which is only a few metres away. Continue descending on the loose, stony ground with views towards the Kyrenia range, and after a very steep downhill section arrive at a junction with an **information board**.

Continue left, uphill beneath pine trees. At first the views are obstructed by the trees and bushes but soon Pedoulas village and the surrounding mountains appear on your right.

Follow the path with enchanting views for about 20min and arrive at a small wooden **bridge**. Continue on the undulating path for another 20min or so. When the path splits, keep right and a few minutes later arrive at a

Trees are sparse on the stony mountainside, giving plenty of opportunity to marvel at the panorama.

Dried-out tree: one of many natural 'statues' scattered on the hillside

dirt track with a blank information board. Go left on the dirt track and about 10min later leave it to the right on a path downhill.

Soon cross another wooden **bridge**. You might notice a faint path on the right, but keep straight on the well-trodden path and then some buildings (**Kampi tou Kalogirou**) appear on the right. Soon pass by a playground; there is a restaurant to the left on the other side of the road. Arrive at an information board and go left on the asphalt road (F828). Walk past the restaurant and at the roundabout go towards Troodos (F952 road). Follow the winding asphalt road for 3.5km to arrive back at **Prodromos Dam picnic site**.

WALK 12
Kannoures Trail

Start	800m from Agios Nikolaos tis Stegis church on the F936 road (N34.97791, E32.88517)
Finish	Troodos Square
Distance	10km (6¾ miles)kannoures trail
Ascent/Descent	1050m/210m
Grade	3
Time	4hr 30min
Refreshments	Restaurants and shops in Troodos Square
Access	From the direction of Troodos village on the B9 road, before reaching Kakopetria, turn left onto F936. Follow this winding road to Agios Nikolaos tis Stegis church. (It is possible to park in the church car park but check the opening hours (see below), as the gate is shut outside of visiting times.) From the church, follow the tarmac (F936) road for about 800m. There is space for parking by the nature trail sign at the beginning of the walk.
Note	The walk is intended as a one-way route; it is best to arrange a taxi from Troodos Square back to the start point before setting out.

Like a secret gem, the gorge that holds the Karkotis river is hidden by the mountains of Troodos. For a number of kilometres the scenery on this walk is dominated by rocks, pine trees, boulders and the river. The path crosses the rushing stream countless times, often on slippery rocks, in the picturesque gorge. There is the possibility of seeing the endemic mouflon hopping on rocks and birds swooping between pine trees as you make your way through this magical ravine.

AGIOS NIKOLAOS TIS STEGIS

Also known as 'St Nicholas of the Roof', its name refers to the second timber roof which was added to protect the building from snow. The Byzantine church was part of a monastery built in the 11th century; the narthex, dome and second roof were added a few hundred years later. Apart from the church, no other buildings of the monastery survived.

Wall paintings – dating from at least five different centuries – cover the entire interior and the church is listed as a UNESCO World Heritage Site.

Visiting hours: Tuesday–Saturday, 9am–4pm; Sunday, 11am–4pm; closed on Mondays and public holidays.

The trail starts as a wide forest track on the left side of the F936 road about 800m from Agios Nikolaos tis Stegis church. The start is marked with a 'Nature Trail Agios Nikolaos – Kannoures 9km' sign.

The wide forest track winds uphill on the mountainside with views to Kakopetria on the left. About 300m from the road, pass by a fenced area where you can see some of the old buildings of a former mine in the valley. There are green walking signs along the dirt track, and about 40min after leaving the tarmac road a sign marks a narrow path on the left.

Follow this footpath on the mountainside with occasional views to the surrounding rocky mountains. Curve around rocks with views to a captivating ravine on the left and soon walk between boulders closer to the rushing stream. Half an hour after leaving the wide dirt track, cross the stream for the first time and then climb steadily

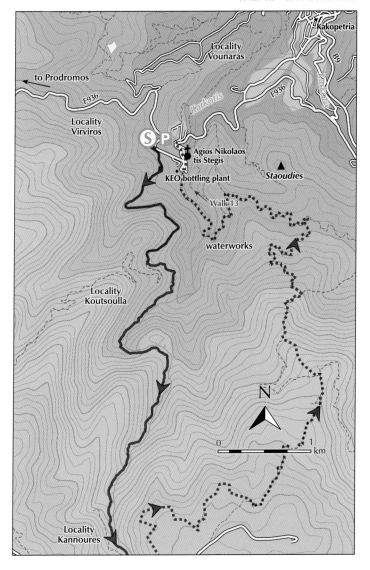

The crossings are often on slippery rocks: select your crossing points carefully because the water is deep and the flow can be rapid in places.

uphill by the river. A giant rock towers on the right as the rocky path makes its way deeper into the gorge.

Less then 10min after the first crossing, cross the stream again. For the next couple of hours you will follow the stream on the rough footpath and cross the water myriad times. ◄

The rugged path runs steadily uphill. Pine trees are the main vegetation in the gorge, but sometimes they are completely absent, leaving only the barren mountainside and the sound of rushing water. The narrow path is easy to follow but occasionally you may have to alter your way and walk upstream a bit to find a better crossing place.

A small rushing waterfall in the picturesque gorge

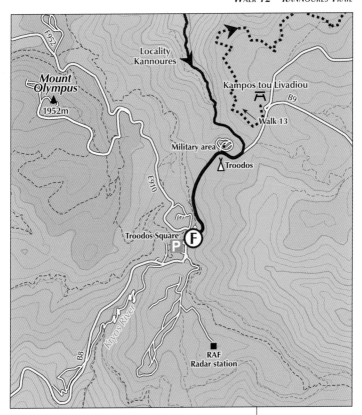

A little more then an hour into the endless crossings, the stream divides and a narrow path runs on the mountainside with a drop on the left. ▶ Hop over some gullies and from around the 6km mark there are more pine trees clinging onto the rocky mountainside.

The path winds relentlessly uphill with huge rocks on the left. Continue climbing and cross the stream a few more times before a wide forest track becomes visible on the other side of the streambed. Soon the path bends right, crosses the river and joins a forest track. Turn left

As you zigzag uphill around the 5km mark, stop and look back to admire a scenic panorama of the plains and the beginning of the Kyrenia range.

Towering rocks hug the river along the trail

and continue on the wide, rugged forest track, which follows the narrowing stream. A few minutes later cross the now very narrow and shallow stream for the last time. Pass by some young pine trees and reach the tarmac road (B9). Turn right and follow this road for 1.2km to arrive at **Troodos Square**, from where you can either retrace your steps (although this would make a very long outing) or take a taxi back to the start.

WALK 13
Mnimata Piskopon Trail

Start	Kampos tou Livadiou picnic site (N34.93607, E32.88959)
Finish	Agios Nikolaos tis Stegis church
Distance	13km (8 miles)
Ascent/Descent	350m/1220m
Grade	3
Time	4hr
Refreshments	None along the way. Cafés and restaurants in Troodos Square.
Access	The nature trail starts on the left side of the B9 road about 1.5km from Troodos Square towards Karvounas. Parking available nearby.
Note	This is intended as a one-way route; while retracing your steps from Agios Nikolaos tis Stegis is possible, it would make a long day with a steep climb on the return. It is best to arrange a taxi before setting out.

The first section of this walk follows a very well maintained nature trail offering excellent views to Mt Olympus – Cyprus' highest peak. The narrow path beneath pine trees occasionally joins forest tracks, and after a leisurely start it goes steeply downhill on loose ground. As you descend you will have breathtaking views towards Kakopetria village, the Madari ridge and Morphou Bay.

Marked trails are indicated just off the B9 road, where there is space to park. The Mnimata Piskopon Trail is signposted and a few metres further on there is an information board illustrating two different trails: take the No2 trail, to the left. A few minutes later pass a picnic site on the right, as views to the houses of Troodos village and a weather station appear on the left.

As the path narrows, the ski lifts on the slopes of Mt Olympus can be spotted and the deep Karkotis river gorge can be admired on your left. ◄ The path bends slightly to the right, and as you descend among mighty black pines and endemic golden oaks you will get close to the gorge again. Just before the 2km mark, a dirt track joins in from the right; keep straight on and follow the widening path, which bends away from the gorge.

About 40–45min into the walk, the No2 trail turns left and about 100m later arrives at a junction. Continue straight on, towards Kakopetria. The path swings on the mountainside and crosses a little gully before turning back on itself. As it winds on the hillside for about 15–20min there are ravishing views on the left. Arrive at an intersection, turn left onto the cairn-marked forest track and you'll soon spot E4 signs on some of the trees. A few minutes later, at a clearing with a bench, the

The ground is a bit loose and cambered and can be slippery, so don't let the beautiful views take all your attention away!

View of the Madari ridge from the trail

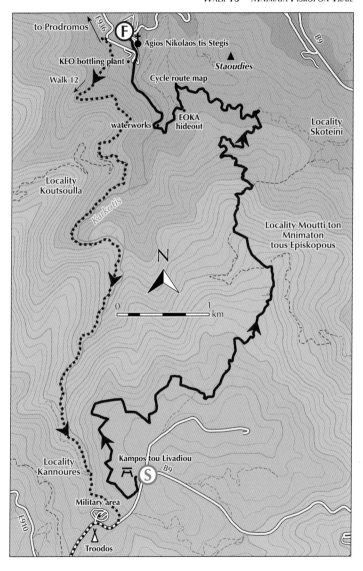

to Prodromos

F1936

F

Agios Nikolaos tis Stegis

KEO bottling plant

Staoudies

Cycle route map

Walk 12

B9

EOKA
hideout

Locality
Skoteini

waterworks

Karkotis

Locality
Koutsoulla

Locality Moutti ton
Mnimaton
tous Episkopous

N

0   1 km

Locality
Kannoures

Kampos tou Livadiou

S

B9

Military area

E910

Troodos

No2 track bends right. When it joins a dirt road, bear left towards Kakopetria.

Continue downhill with views to pine-dotted rocky mountainsides and the first glimpse of the distant Adelfoi (Madari) peak. There are occasional E4 marks on some trees, and soon the E4 leaves the track to the right. This is a short-cut as a few minutes later it rejoins the track, where you keep right. Approximately 100m further on, at a junction where the E4 heads to Platania, continue straight on towards Kakopetria. From here the path runs steeply downhill. You will see the remains of some steps, and the ground is very loose and slippery as you descend. ◄

About 20min after leaving the E4 trail, arrive at a dirt track. Keep right downhill and about 70m later the path leaves the dirt road to the right. Continue downhill on a very steep, rough and loose path with some deteriorated steps and then walk in the shade of trees for a while. Descend steeply for about 45min, mainly on stony, crumbly ground with excellent views to the mountains and Kakopetria.

Not long before reaching a dirt road the path becomes sandy with scattered stones. Arrive at the dirt road with 'Agios Nikolaos 3km' and 'Platania 5km' signs. Go left towards Agios Nikolaos and at the next junction keep straight on. Follow the 'number 1' cycle route, which goes in the same direction for about 1.8km.

Ignore the track on the right as you arrive at a bench and a **cycle route map**. About 250m later, when the track turns right, spot 'hideout 1&2' signs on the left. ◄ Soon after a bend the cycle route leaves the track to the right; continue straight on and 500m later arrive at a **waterworks** building where you cross the rushing Karkotis river. About 700m later you reach the end of the dirt track; go right on the concrete road and follow it to the Agios Nikolaos tis Stegis church.

The Byzantine **Agios Nikolaos tis Stegis church** was part of a monastery built in the 11th century; its narthex, dome and second roof were added a few hundred years later. The church is the only surviving

There are views to Mt Olympus on the left and soon you have a direct view to Kakopetria, a football pitch, Cape Kormakitis and Morphou Bay.

You can make a detour to visit one of them via a small path on a bend.

building of the monastery complex, and its interior wall paintings have won it a place on the UNESCO World Heritage List.

Visiting hours: Tuesday–Saturday, 9am–4pm; Sunday, 11am–4pm; closed on Mondays and public holidays.

Having visited the church you can either retrace your steps (bearing in mind that this would involve a steep climb) or take a taxi back to the picnic site at the start.

WALK 14
Atalante Trail

Start/Finish	Troodos Square (N34.92424, E32.88082)
Distance	14km (8¾ miles)
Ascent/Descent	625m/625m
Grade	2
Time	4hr–4hr 30min
Refreshments	Restaurants and souvenir shops on Troodos Square
Access	Troodos Square can be accessed from the B8 and B9 roads. There is a large car park at the start point.

A well signposted, narrow, stony path cut into a mountainside runs around Mt Olympus, with impressive views along the way. It is a comfortable walk beneath pines and without strenuous ascent. Despite the length of the trail, many people take it to admire the panorama. Yet there are sections where you find yourself alone and can enjoy the rustling trees and birdsong. This walk is most enjoyable on a clear day.

Atalante is a renowned and swift-footed huntress in Greek mythology. Her father wanted a son, and when she was born she was left in the woods to die. However, Atalante was found and looked after by a

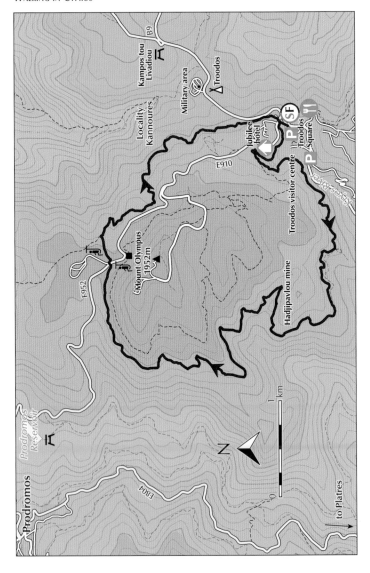

bear. Growing up, she spent lot of time with hunters and became the best of them.

The signposted trail starts at the end of the boardwalk by the playground next to the main road. The well-trodden path runs beneath pine trees on the hillside and soon past the **Jubilee Hotel** on the right. Cross a dry streambed and continue to the left, passing the **Troodos Visitor Centre** from above.

The well-used, narrow – sometimes exposed – path continues on the side of Mt Olympus with a rock wall towering on the right. The snaking road between Platres and Troodos is on the left down below and there are stunning views towards the south coast.

MT OLYMPUS

Mt Olympus (known locally as Chionistra – 'the snowy one') at 1952m is the highest mountain in Cyprus. Its highest point can't be accessed as a British long-range radar operates from its peak. However, some of the most popular and enjoyable trails with magnificent views are on its pine-covered mountainside. Europe's most southerly ski resorts are on Mt Olympus' slopes. People started skiing in Cyprus in 1934, and in 1947 the Cyprus Ski Club was established. After a first ski lift on the eastern side of the mountain, the second ski lift started operating west of Troodos in 1951.

A narrow path cut into Olympus' mountainside

After the 2km mark the vegetation becomes denser and you walk between bushes and pine trees for a while. About 30–40min after leaving Troodos Square, the narrow footpath meets another path; continue straight on by a bench with an iron arrow indicating the direction.

Pine trees obstruct the view for a while. Cross a little stream and then arrive at a fountain with running water at the 3km mark. After the fountain there is a clear view again on the left and a sheer rocky mountainside scattered with pine trees towering on the right. Soon spot a terraced reforestation area on the far left, as well as the tops of the two radar domes on a nearby mountain. About 20min after the fountain the path joins into a wider track; keep right and soon the track narrows back into a path.

Follow the contour of the mountainside with fantastic views on the left and a rocky slope soaring on the right, and then at around the 5km mark the path arrives at the disused **Hadjipavlou chromium mine**.

The **mine** has been closed since 1982 and there is a fence in front of the entrance. The roof of the tunnel has collapsed in places, but standing at the entrance you can feel the cold, damp air drifting out.

As the path sharply doubles back on itself, look back to see the entrance of the mine.

After the mine as you continue by a rock face you might hear a thin gurgling stream on your left down below. Soon another path joins in; keep left, cross a stream and then walk by pines and cypress trees. ◄ The trail is exposed in places as it swings around rocks.

At around 7km note a huge **sign**: 'Carelessness of visitors caused the fire', which refers to a forest fire but doesn't give information about the damage or the year when it happened. Pines stand grandly on the battle-scarred hillside regardless.

Soon the view slightly changes, and on the left the distant houses of Prodromos dominate the panorama as you walk through pine forest. At around the 8km mark you'll see the top of Mt Olympus on the right, and 1km later as you walk by juniper trees the road is clearly visible.

The path widens and soon arrives at a noticeboard and a stone building by a tarmac road. Cross the road by the information board. There is a parking area slightly to your right; head towards the electricity pole and the trail continues on a dirt track to the left.

Walk with a drop on your right, noting a building on the hill on the left. A few minutes later leave the track on a narrow path to the right and descend into a ravine, and then ascend on occasional stone steps. At the 12km mark the path joins a dirt track; continue downhill to the left as an iron arrow indicates.

Walk on the mountainside with the ravine on your left and about 600m later another forest track joins in. Keep right as an arrow indicates. Down below on the left an impressive gorge can be seen with the hidden Kannoures trail, and in the distance Kakopetria village. Leave the dirt track to the right as an arrow indicates and about 15min later arrive back at **Troodos Square**.

Europe's most southerly ski resort is in the Troodos mountains

WALK 15
Artemis Trail

Start/Finish	Troodos Square (N34.92424, E32.88082)
Alternative start/ finish	Car park on F953 road (N34.93304, E32.87216)
Distance	12km (7½ miles); from alternative start (official Artemis Trail): 7km (4½ miles)
Ascent/Descent	430m/430m; from alternative start: 280m/280m
Grade	2; from alternative start: 1
Time	3hr 40min; from alternative start: 2hr 30min
Refreshments	Cafés and restaurants at Troodos Square
Access	Troodos Square can be accessed from the B8 and B9 roads. Alternative start is on F953 road about 300m from the Troodos–Prodromos road (E910). There is a large car park at the start point.

Like an older sister, the Artemis Trail looks over to the Atalante Trail from a higher altitude. The trail is considerably shorter than the Atalante Trail, however by starting from Troodos Square, first briefly following the Atalante Trail and then joining the Artemis trail after about 2km, the distance is lengthened to 12km. The signposted path runs on the rocky hillside with ravishing views while it passes the ski lifts on the slopes of Mt Olympus.

> **Artemis** was the goddess of hunting, natural environment and virginity. When she was born she helped her mother to deliver her twin brother Apollo, and became the protector of childbirth and labour.

From Troodos Square, the signposted Atalante Trail begins by an information board at the end of a boardwalk located by the playground next to the main road. The well-trodden path runs beneath pine trees on the hillside and soon passes the **Jubilee Hotel** on the right. Cross a dry streambed and continue to the left, and a few minutes

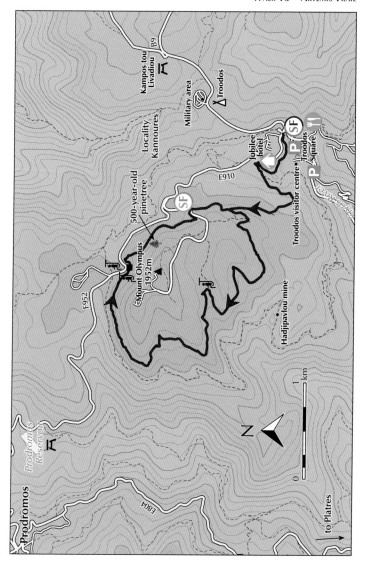

later the path splits; the Atalante Trail is marked with an arrow and goes to the left, but keep to the right on the unmarked trail running slightly uphill. Walk along the stony path on the rocky slope with views to pine-covered mountains and soon the buildings of Troodos are visible on the left.

As the path bends right, ignore the track joining from the left and carry straight on. About 45min from Troodos Square, after a gentle uphill section, arrive at a dirt track, which is where you join the Artemis Trail. Keep left as the iron arrow indicates.

A narrow section of the Artemis Trail snakes between exposed rocks and steep drops

Alternative start/official Artemis Trail

In the car park on the F953 road there is an information board where the Artemis Trail officially starts. Take the path by the board and walk on the rocky hillside. A few minutes later reach a junction: keep straight on as the iron arrow indicates.

Walk on the mountainside beneath pine trees with views to the left. About 5min after the iron arrow at the junction, cross a forest track and continue on its other side. For the next 30–40min follow the path on the rocky mountainside through pine forest, often with stunning views to the left.

Emerge onto a dirt road and continue left. Pass a **ski lift** and as the path bends to the left you pass a building. Once again, follow the narrow path on the rocky mountainside with stunning views on your left. ▸ You'll see the peak of Mt Olympus with the radar dome as you walk through black pine forest.

The stony path runs on the sometimes barren mountainside with rocks towering on the right, and soon a snaking tarmac road comes into view.

An hour after passing the first ski slope, arrive at a green-roofed restaurant building and ski lifts. The path continues in-between the building and a lift, getting very close to the tarmac road. After the building, the path swings away from the road and runs slightly uphill.

Walk through pine forest and shortly arrive at a 500-year-old giant black **pine**. Carry straight on and very soon pass under another ski lift cable. Arrive at a forest track and a few metres later leave it to the left. Join the path and shortly afterwards reach a tarmac road with an information board which is the official start of the Artemis Trail – and the end of the walk for those using the alternative start/finish point.

If you started from Troodos Square, continue on the path by the information board. Walk on the rocky hillside and a few minutes later reach the junction where the trail from Troodos Square joins the Artemis Trail. Go left and retrace your steps to **Troodos Square**.

In the hazy distance the salt lake near Limassol, and then Prodromos village hugged by mountains in the valley can be spotted.

WALK 16
Caledonia circular

Start/Finish	Psilo Dendro restaurant, Pano Platres (N34.89586, E32.86863)
Distance	9km (5½ miles)
Ascent/Descent	570m/570m
Grade	2
Time	3hr
Refreshments	Restaurants in Platres, and Psilo Dendro at start of walk
Access	Psilo Dendro is located on B8 road between Platres and Troodos. Parking available at restaurant.

This is a well-known and popular nature trail by the rushing Kryos river – one of the few rivers in Cyprus that carries water all year round. The best time to see the waterfall is probably during the spring months when the most water is cascading down. The clear and well-maintained shady path crosses the river mainly on bridges. The second part of the trail takes you across a pine-covered mountainside with impressive views along the way. The final section of the trail is the first section of Walk 17 (Pouziaris Trail) in reverse.

The nature trail starts by the information board at the restaurant car park. From here, walk straight up alongside the fence on a concrete road to the next information board. Follow the well-trodden, rocky footpath beneath trees and between huge rocks by the Kryos river, and soon reach the first bridge.

Walking between golden oaks, cross the rushing river several times on wooden bridges. After about half an hour, reach the **Caledonia Falls** where the ice-cold water comes crashing down from rocks at a height of 13m.

The **Caledonia Falls** were named by Scots who visited the Platres area in 1878. They named the

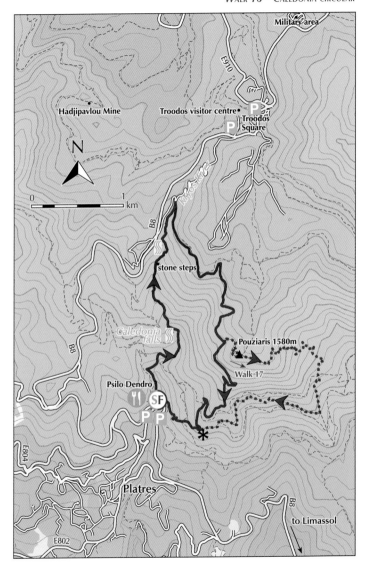

Military area

Hadjipavlou Mine

Troodos visitor centre

P

P Troodos
Square

E910

N

0   1
km

B8

Kryos Potamos

stone steps

Caledonia
falls

B8

Pouziaris 1580m

Walk 17

Psilo Dendro

SF

P P

*

E804

Platres

to Limassol

B8

E802

105

waterfall after their homeland: Caledonia was the
Latin name for Scotland, given by the Romans.

Many people follow the river upstream only to the
waterfall, however the trail continues. After the waterfall
continue on the path and ascend the steep steps. At the
top of Caledonia Falls, go over another bridge and then
continue slightly uphill. The path might be muddy and
slippery here and you will have to cross the river on rocks
a few more times. ◄

The path progresses steadily uphill, and about 30min
after leaving Caledonia Falls you arrive at a set of very

*The sound of rushing
water accompanies
you as you walk
upstream amid the
moss-covered rocks.*

*Rewarding views
towards the south
on the return route*

steep **stone steps** with railings. Just before the top of the steps there is a viewpoint where you can catch your breath and admire the water gushing down on rocks. Soon, nearing the old Troodos–Platres road, the water gently runs over and around smaller rocks.

Emerge onto a road by an information board. Go right on the track marked 'E4' and signposted for Pouziaris. Follow the forest track beneath pine trees for about 15min then leave it to the right on a narrow path as the sign indicates. (The E4-marked track continues straight on.) As the path follows the contour of the mountainside, there are fewer pine trees and more fine views towards the south coast and the village of Platres down below.

The rocky path descends beneath kermes oaks (*Quercus coccifera*) and pines and occasionally gets very narrow and loose. About 40min after leaving the forest track there is a narrow path on the left. ▶ Continue straight on downhill: this part of the trail is the first section of the Pouziaris Trail from Psilo Dendro.

This path goes up to Pouziaris peak as part of Walk 17 Pouziaris Trail.

Walk on the mountainside with huge rocks towering on the left and stunning views on the right. You soon start to descend but this time the views are obstructed by trees. Reach a forest track and then continue on its other side slightly to the left. Soon, at a junction, bear right and follow the sign to Psilo Dendro. A few minutes later there is a final opportunity to admire the views at a **viewpoint** from rocks.

About 10min after the previous one, cross another forest track and continue on its other side straight on downhill. Take a few steps and after a steep downhill section on loose surface zigzag back to **Psilo Dendro**.

WALK 17
Pouziaris Trail

Start/Finish	Psilo Dendro restaurant, Pano Platres (N34.89586, E32.86863)
Distance	9km (5½ miles)
Ascent/Descent	610m/610m
Grade	2
Time	3hr
Refreshments	Restaurants in Platres, and Psilo Dendro at start of walk
Access	Psilo Dendro is located on B8 road between Platres and Troodos. Parking available at restaurant.

The narrow, rocky path cut into the hillside climbs up to Pouziaris peak where memorable views welcome you. It then runs mainly downhill with more grand views along the way. Diverse scenery accompanies you during this pleasant walk on pine-covered slopes. The first hour of the walk is the final section of Walk 16 (Caledonia Trail) in reverse.

Starting from the Psilo Dendro car park, keep left on the main road (B8). The trail begins a few metres away on the left, at the Pouziaris Trail information board. The path starts zigzagging steeply uphill through pine forest and about 10min later it reaches a track. Cross over the track and continue on its other side, straight uphill.

Soon reach a junction with a 'Psilo Dendro 1km' sign. (You will return to this junction from the path on the right.) Keep left towards Troodos Square. Cross another forest track and continue on its other side, bearing left slightly. Ascend steadily beneath trees at first and then walk on the mountainside with rocks towering on the right and great views on the left.

About an hour after starting the trail, turn right uphill on a narrow, stony path and soon climb amid kermes oaks. ◄ The ground becomes less rough and it might be

The path going straight on is Walk 16 (Caledonia Trail).

108

Tall pine trees tower over the path on Pouziaris

covered with dry pine needles as you climb among giant pines. Make the final ascent on a stony path to reach **Pouziaris peak** (1580m) 10–15min after the junction where you turned right.

Take a rest after your climb and enjoy the excellent scenery from the **summit of Pouziaris**. On a clear day, the panorama unfolds from the red roofs of the houses of Platres to the coastline, often bathed in hazy sunshine. Even the outline of Limassol can be spotted in the blurred distance.

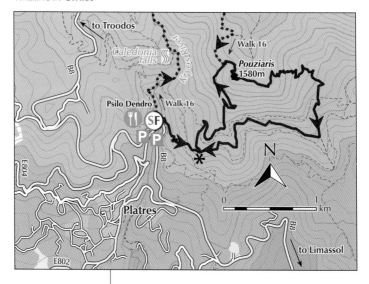

Continue on the path, and at a junction go right and downhill as the 'Psilo Dendro (6.5km)' sign indicates. As the vegetation thins out, excellent views accompany you on the right, while a rocky mountainside dominates on the left. The path winds its way slightly uphill to a junction where you keep straight and then start to descend.

As you zigzag downhill the views are ever-changing, from the peak with two radar domes in front of you to the surrounding mountains, and towards the coast to the south. About 45min after leaving Pouziaris peak the path widens a bit and meets a disused, overgrown track from the right – but carry straight on as the sign indicates.

Descend steeply on an uneven rocky path and turn sharply right where indicated by a huge sign. Shortly, cross a forest track and continue straight downhill on its opposite side. Follow the curve of the mountain gently downhill; soon cross a dry streambed and then walk over huge rocks. The path then smoothes out and carries on downhill before running very gently uphill for about a kilometre.

After crossing two rockfalls the route starts to descend again. Emerge onto a forest track and continue on its other side downhill. At around 8km there are still views towards Limassol and you arrive back at the junction with the 'Psilo Dendro 1km' sign. Continue as indicated.

Soon cross a forest track and continue on its other side, straight downhill. Take a few steps down, and after a steep downhill section zigzag back to **Psilo Dendro**.

WALK 18
Loymata ton Aeton Trail

Start/Finish	Amiantos playground (N34.92019, E32.93310)
Distance	4km (2½ miles)
Ascent/Descent	190m/190m
Grade	1
Time	1hr 30min
Refreshments	Taverns in Amiantos village
Access	From the direction of Limassol, follow the B8 towards Troodos and take the E801 to Amiantos after the village of Trimiklini. Parking available at playground.

This short but spectacular walk starts from the edge of Amiantos village and initially follows a stream, which it crosses a few times before reaching a point where there is the opportunity to climb up to an EOKA hideout. The second part of the trail runs along hillside with some great views towards the river gorge.

Follow the stony road leading uphill with the stream on your right and a few minutes later arrive at another dirt road where there are water tanks on the right. An information board (actually a blank wooden board without any information at the time of writing) marks the beginning of the path, which starts to the left between golden oaks.

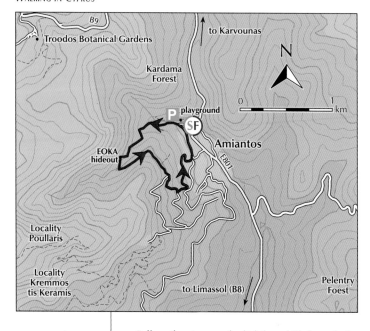

Follow the stony path slightly uphill through the gorge with the stream on your right. Soon cross the stream over rocks and then continue slightly uphill with a rocky mountainside towering on your right.

Occasional painted red arrows indicate the way. Pass by boulders and soon cross the stream again. Continue between myrtle (*Myrtus communis*) and golden oaks and shortly reach a sign: 'hideout'. On the right, a narrow, steep path with worn steps leads up to a small **EOKA hideout**. ◄ Climb up to the hideout and then descend back to the path, which continues through the gorge.

Soon cross the stream again and walk alongside the gurgling water. All too soon the path bends to the left and leaves the stream. A painted red arrow marks the turn; the path seems to continue straight on for a bit as well, but there is a line of stones 'closing' it, indicating that you shouldn't go that way.

EOKA fighters used these hideouts in the mountains between 1955 and 1959.

112

The outward route from Amiantos follows a stream

There are some stone steps as you climb between pines and golden oaks, and soon a view to the gorge on your left. Then the path swings away from the gorge and starts to descend.

When you reach a dirt track, go straight uphill as the painted red arrow indicates and a few minutes later arrive at a junction. Go downhill, slightly left, and a few minutes later reach a tarmac road. Go left, and shortly reach another tarmac road. Keep left again and carry straight on all the way back to the **playground**.

WALK 19
Madari Trail

Start/Finish	Locality Doxa Soi o Theos information board (N34.95593, E32.96294)
Distance	13km (8 miles); including Teisia tis Madaris extension: 16.5km (10¼ miles)
Ascent/Descent	900m/900m; including extension: 1080m/1080m
Grade	3
Time	5hr; including extension: 6hr
Refreshments	None
Access	Arriving from the direction of Karvounas village on the E909 road, turn left onto the F944 road just before Kyperounta village. Pass the 'Adventure Mountain Park' and there is a parking area on the left-hand side of the road, opposite the Locality Doxa Soi o Theos information board.

The well-trodden path goes initially steeply uphill and then there are some gentle undulating sections as you head towards the Madari fire lookout station. Enjoy the splendid 360-degree panorama from a viewpoint. The trail can then be extended with the short Teisia tis Madaris Trail, from where you can observe an impressive example of a sheeted dike complex. From the fire lookout station the trail runs mainly downhill and from Locality Selladi tou Karamanli it is part of the E4 European Long Distance Trail.

Follow the path that starts by the information board and then zigzags steeply uphill between golden oaks, rock roses and pines. Almost immediately you have some views to the left, but this is just a taster as even better views await you during the walk. The path climbs steadily uphill and about 15min after leaving Locality Doxa Soi o Theos you have the first views to the right towards Amiantos and Troodos. The path bends gently left and soon allows fine views to the Madari (Adelfoi) peak in the distance.

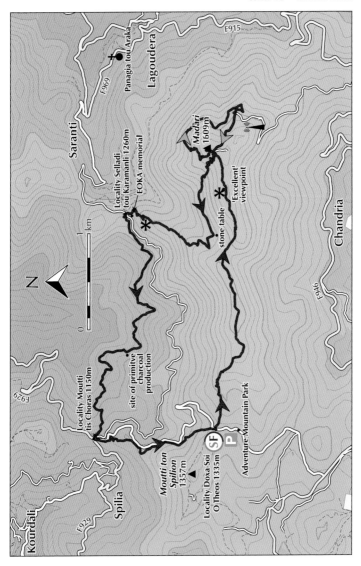

There is a small building at the top of Madari, which is one of the 13 **fire lookout stations** located on some of the highest peaks of Cyprus. From May to October, when the risk of fire is high, these lookouts are manned around the clock. The fire-watcher is familiar with the area, as he usually comes from a local village and can locate the fire and guide the firemen accurately.

The Kyrenia mountain range, Morfou Bay and the north coast are easily visible on a clear day.

Continue on the sometimes narrow path with views to the cultivated slopes of Kyperounta village on the right-hand side. An hour into the walk you'll reach an '**Excellent Viewpoint**' sign: there is a short detour from here to the mountain top, where you can enjoy a magnificent 360-degree panorama. ◀ Drink in the view, return to the path and continue along the ridge.

About 10min later arrive at a junction with an information board near the fire lookout station. At this junction you have several choices: as well as continuing on the main route, you can walk up a steep, concrete path to the fire lookout building from where there are views towards the mountains and Nicosia/Lefkoşa, the Kyrenia

Benches are located on some of the best viewing spots along the way

mountain range and the recognisable radar dome on the peak of Machairas. There is also an option to extend your walk on the 3.5km-long Teisia tis Madaris Trail.

Extension: Teisia tis Madaris Trail

The signposted Teisia tis Madaris Trail starts from the information board which describes some of the geological characteristics, such as sheeted dikes, that can be observed in this area.

At first the narrow path curves steeply downhill on the rocky mountainside, which soon becomes rich with vegetation. ▸ You can make a detour to a viewpoint with a bench not long after the start of the trail, but the path continues downhill, often with great views to the left and with huge rocks towering on the right-hand side.

The views change on your left as the path curves around the **Madari peak**. There is a tiny village down below, and then from a viewpoint you might be able to spot the roof of the Panagia tou Araka church in Lagoudera. Continue, taking in the mountain views on your left. There is a gentle uphill section and then just after the 2km mark the path splits; go right uphill (the

On this circular route overgrown nature labels describe various plants.

Madari fire lookout station

117

other path leads towards the antennas) and a few minutes later emerge onto a dirt road. Turn right and walk back to the junction near the fire lookout station.

To continue on the main route, from the junction, follow the path downhill marked 'Doxa Soi o Theos 9.2km'. ◄ Pines and golden oaks are the main vegetation as you zigzag downhill with views to the right. Like a grey river dashing down the mountainside, deposits of talus rock (rocky debris) cross the path, and in springtime pink rock roses give a dash of bright colour. As you descend, enjoy the fantastic views on the right-hand side.

The name Doxa Soi o Theos is spelled slightly differently on the signs, eg 'Doxa si o Theos'.

About half an hour after leaving the junction near the fire lookout station, reach a **stone table** with stools in the shade of pines next to the path. As the path bends right you can glimpse the fire lookout building on the peak of Madari in the distance on the right. About 50–60min after starting the descent from the fire lookout station, notice a wooden arrow with a sign in Greek pointing to a path by a bench. This takes you to a viewpoint. From the wooden sign, continue downhill and 10min later arrive at **Locality Selladi tou Karamanli** (1260m). ◄

There is an EOKA monument close to the map board.

Emerging onto a dirt track, the trail continues downhill on its other side, by the 'Doxa Soi o Theos 5.6km' sign. As you walk downhill, the hillside is scattered with moss-covered rocks beneath golden oaks. Walk across two deposits of talus rock and soon you will see the first E4 sign, indicating that you are now on part of the long-distance trail.

The villages of Agia Eirini and Kannavia nestle in a valley on your right. Pass a **site of primitive charcoal production**, then the path widens a bit and soon joins a forest track. Go right as the E4 sign indicates and a few minutes later arrive at another forest track. The path continues on the other side of this track, a few metres uphill to the left. Shortly emerge onto a tarmac road and on its other side there is an information board. Arrive at **Locality Moutti tis Choras** about an hour after leaving Locality Selladi tou Karamanli.

Follow the 'Doxa Soi o Theos 1.8km' sign. Take the road signposted E4 towards Kyperounta and about 50m later leave the tarmac road to the right as the sign indicates. Follow the path marked E4, between the dirt track and the tarmac road. The path runs mainly parallel to the tarmac road with some views between the tree crowns to the mountains. ▶ Continue steadily uphill and about 30min after Locality Moutti tis Choras emerge onto a tarmac road, turn right and a few metres later arrive back at **Locality Doxa Soi o Theos**.

On the right is Spilia village, with the fire lookout station on Madari to the left in the distance.

WALK 20

Kannavia circular

Start/Finish	Kannavia village, at junction of F929 road and Andrea Patsalidi Street (N34.98073, E32.97637)
Distance	19km (11¾ miles)
Ascent/Descent	1310/1310m
Grade	3
Time	5hr 30min–6hr (+ allow minimum 1hr to explore the EOKA headquarters)
Refreshments	Water may be found at Locality Straorouthkias but take plenty with you.
Access	Kannavia is located on the F929 road, 10km from the B9. Roadside parking in the village.

This long walk connects three nature trails and a section of the E4, and at times also follows dirt tracks. The first 3km is a strenuous climb with outstanding views. Along the way, take time to enjoy a peaceful, hidden viewpoint where you can hear birdsong and admire the grand mountains. There is an opportunity to visit the EOKA headquarters on the hill above Spilia before descending to Agia Eirini. The final short section of the walk follows a tarmac road connecting Agia Eirini with Kannavia village.

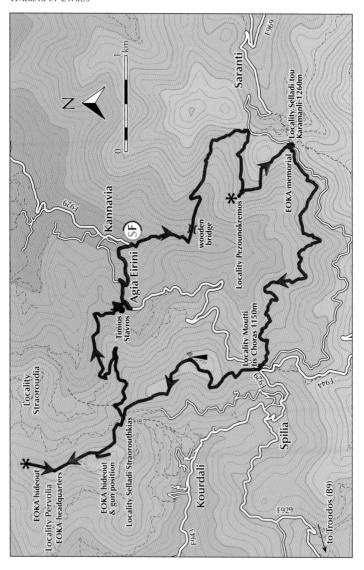

The trail starts from the information board on Andrea Patsalidi Street in Kannavia. Go downhill and a few metres later reach 28th Oktourion Street, where the 'Selladi tou Karamanli' sign with an arrow indicates the direction.

Walk along the wide track with a valley on your left for about 600m, then a path – marked 'Selladi tou Karamanli' – starts to the left. Go downhill on this narrow path and almost immediately cross over a small bridge and continue uphill on the other side. There are some wooden steps by a small cultivated piece of land on the slope but soon you climb between golden oaks and pines.

Cross a rocky streambed, and as the path climbs higher from the valley, rock roses appear between the

After crossing a bridge, the route runs through dense forest

121

There are great views to Agia Eirini and Kannavia villages as well as to the Madari peak.

pines and golden oaks. Zigzag steeply uphill on the narrow path for about an hour with rewarding views to the pine-covered mountains and the valley. ◄

After an hour of strenuous climbing from Kannavia, arrive at a road. The 'Selladi tou Karamanli' sign with an arrow suggests walking on the road, but you can get to Selladi tou Karamanli along a narrow and picturesque path which starts on the right.

Walk slightly downhill between golden oaks and pines and as the path swings around the mountain you can enjoy the views. ◄ About 15min from the tarmac road, arrive at **Locality Pezounokremos** where a sign indicates a viewpoint 130m away. If you make the detour to this roofed viewpoint you will be rewarded with a 180-degree panorama of the mountains and the valley.

Like tiny model houses on a giant plotting board, the buildings of Agia Eirini and Kannavia nestle in the valley.

From the viewpoint, retrace your steps to Locality Pezounokremos and continue to the right. Follow the less-used, stony path curving around the edge of the mountainside, going slightly uphill for about 30min to arrive at **Locality Selladi tou Karamanli**. There is an EOKA monument on the hillside, to the right of an information board.

EOKA

EOKA (Ethniki Organosi tou Kyprakou Agona – National Organisation of Cypriot Fighters) was founded in 1955 and its main aim was to end the British rule and achieve enosis (union) with Greece. The founder and leader of the organisation was Georgios Grivas, who managed the first EOKA operations from Nicosia/Lefkoşa but then joined his team in the Troodos mountains. The second-in-command of the organisation was Grigoris Afxentiou. Between 1955 and 1959 EOKA targeted the British, and 371 British servicemen lost their lives.

EOKA didn't achieve enosis but the independent Republic of Cyprus was born in 1960.

As a walker you can see numerous hideouts in the mountains, as well as monuments in villages, as the young men who lost their lives as EOKA fighters are remembered as heroes by Greek Cypriots.

Continue sharply to the right towards 'Moutti tis Choras (3.8km)'. As you walk between golden oaks, the slope is scattered with moss-covered rocks. The path winds steadily downhill with views to the right, and about 45min from Selladi tou Karamanli it widens a bit and soon joins a forest track. Keep right and a few minutes later join another forest track. The path, marked 'E4', continues a few metres further uphill to the left.

Emerge onto a tarmac road at a junction with the **Locality Moutti tis Choras** information board. From this junction take the unmarked dirt road on the right. Shortly, when the dirt track splits, keep right. On the left a group of red roofs, the houses of Spilia, break through the greenery of the hills, and as you continue slightly uphill you can enjoy views towards Morfou Bay as well.

When the track splits again, go left (the right track goes up to a radio antenna). From Locality Moutti tis Choras the dirt track curves around the mountainside for 2.5km and arrives at **Locality Selladi Straorouthkias** at a seven-way junction. ▶ As you arrive at the junction, you'll take the first track on the right to continue to Agia Eirini. (From this junction it's about 1hr, mostly downhill,

There is a map board, fountain and picnic area here.

Former armoury near the EOKA headquarters

123

back to Kannavia.) However, before you go down to the village you can visit the hideouts on the hill: take the trail marked 'Hideouts' and zigzag uphill for about 15min.

On the hillside you'll see **hideouts**, **heavy gun positions**, the **EOKA headquarters** and lookouts. Everything is signposted and you can discover the hillside and its history. Follow the 'Headquarters' sign to arrive at the map of the hideouts with a flag mast. From here, follow the 'Hideout No.3' sign to reach to a **viewpoint** where you can enjoy the fantastic panorama of Morfou Bay.

THE BATTLE OF SPILIA

On 12 December 1955, the British Army attempted to encircle the headquarters of the EOKA on the hill near Spilia. The units of Georgios Grivas and Grigoris Afxentiou fought the ascending British troops on the north and south sides of the mountain. There was thick fog on the mountain and the EOKA units managed to escape towards the west. When the British troops reached the summit from opposing sides they couldn't see anything in the fog; thinking they were surrounded by EOKA fighters, they started to shoot each other. The incident led to the highest number of casualties caused by friendly fire during this war.

Retrace your steps to the seven-way junction and continue on the dirt track marked 'To Agia Eirini'. The track swings around the hillside and soon joins another track. Go left downhill. A path signposted 'Agia Eirini' starts from the dirt road on the right. A few stone steps lead downhill between pines, then the path curves around the mountainside with views to the valley and the pine-covered slopes and soon arrives at another dirt track. Go right towards Agia Eirini.

Walk past some cultivated land and then leave the dirt track and continue on a path on the left. Zigzag downhill to **Timios Stavros church** and then continue to the left and meet a tarmac road at **Agia Eirini**. Go right, downhill, and arrive at a junction. Go left, and soon leave Agia Eirini. About 10min later arrive back at **Kannavia** where the walk started.

WALK 21
Asinou Trail

Start/Finish	Cemetery near Agios Theodoros in Solea Valley (N35.04465, E32.92945)
Distance	12km (7½ miles)
Ascent/Descent	540m/540m
Grade	1
Time	4hr
Refreshments	Water at Asinou church and restaurants nearby
Access	On the B9 road from the direction of Kakopetria, turn towards Agios Theodoros on the F975 road. Follow the narrow road through the village and look for an information board on the left. Turn left onto the narrow concrete road by the information board; a few minutes later this reaches a cemetery where there are plenty of places to park.

From the edge of Agios Theodoros village, a narrow path takes you along wooded hillsides to the UNESCO World Heritage-listed 12th-century Asinou church. The barn church is located 3km from Nikitari village and is home to some of the finest Byzantine frescos of the 12th to 17th centuries. This out-and-back trail is well signposted, easy to follow and offers some splendid views towards a bay and the forested mountains.

From the cemetery, the road becomes a dirt road and a few minutes later it splits. Keep left, and as you walk uphill between old almond trees, the landscape before you is dominated by pine-covered mountains.

Shortly leave the dirt track to the left on a path marked 'Palospova alt 520m'. Wooden steps lead up to a narrow path beneath pines. Follow the path along the hillside with great views towards Morfou Bay. About 20–30min after joining the path, reach a dirt track. Go left downhill as indicated by an arrow and a few metres

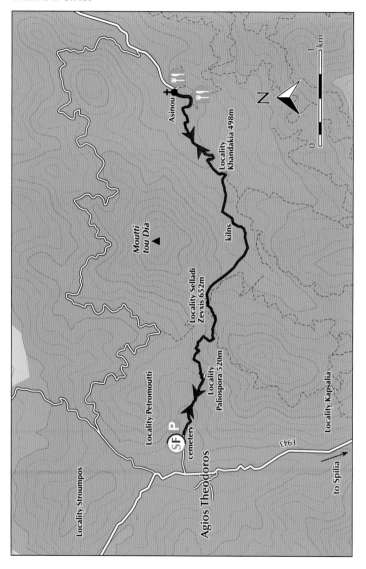

later leave it to the right on a footpath marked 'Asinou 3.6km'.

Continue on the pine-covered hillside and shortly reach **Selladi Zevxis** (altitude 652m) where you can enjoy the panorama of the bay and its surroundings. From here, go downhill on the path, ignoring a track. About 10min after Selladi Zevxis, emerge onto a dirt track and then continue on its other side as indicated by the 'Asinou 2.9km' sign. The path is a bit wider here and the view in front of you is dominated by a towering mountain.

Keep right at the next junction as the sign indicates, and a few metres downhill reach a dirt track. Keep left as the 'Asinou 2.3km' sign indicates. Ignore the track on the left and shortly pass two **kilns** with an information board. Continue on the narrow path with a streambed on your right.

Pine tar was at one time used in pharmaceutics and industry in Cyprus. In the island's forests you'll see many abandoned stone **kilns** which were used to produce tar. Two pits were made – one larger and higher and connected to a smaller pit by a channel.

Tar kilns

Small pieces of wood were layered vertically to fill the bigger pit. It was then covered with mud, moss and ferns and lit from the top through a small opening. As the wood burned, the liquid raw tar flowed from the large pit into the small pit. The tar was then put into smaller wooden moulds/containers.

Pass a water tank and go over a bridge, then turn left at a dirt road. Very soon reach an information board (**Khardakia**, 498m). Bear left on the dirt road; the road becomes tarmac by some buildings and leads to **Asinou church.** ◄

There are some restaurants near the church.

The 12th-century **Asinou church** is home to some of the finest Byzantine frescos. The entire interior of the church is covered with these colourful artworks, which date from the 12th to the 17th century. The building is a UNESCO World Heritage Site.

The beautiful Asinou church

After visiting the church, retrace your steps back to the **cemetery** near Agios Theodoros.

WALK 22

Panagia tou Araka – Stavros tou Agiasmati

Start/Finish	Panagia tou Araka, Lagoudera (N34.96502, E33.00713)
Distance	15km (9¼ miles)
Ascent/Descent	1240m/1240m
Grade	2
Time	5hr–5hr 30min
Refreshments	Water available by Stavros tou Agiasmati church; shop in Lagoudera
Access	From Karvounas on the B9, take the E909 towards Kyperounta and then follow signs to Lagoudera, which is on the F915.

This section of the E4 runs as a nature trail connecting two Byzantine churches, both listed as World Heritage Sites. It is a linear walk in the CTO Nature Trail booklet, but as Stavros tou Agiasmati stands remotely at the end of the trail, you will most probably have to retrace your steps to Lagoudera.

From Lagoudera, you first walk alongside vineyards and almond trees, then the narrow path runs on a forested mountainside with magnificent views.

Stavros tou Agiasmati is closed but you can pre-arrange a visit. Ask for the contact number at one of the CTO offices (see Appendix B).

PANAGIA TOU ARAKA CHURCH

The UNESCO-listed 12th-century church is located just outside of Lagoudera. The name derives from the Greek word *arakas*, or *arakiotissa*, which means wild pea. The church is home to Cyprus' most complete series of frescos from the Middle Byzantine period.

In the 14th century the roof was covered with a protective timber roof. As is typical of the churches in the Troodos, a separate wooden roof covers the dome.

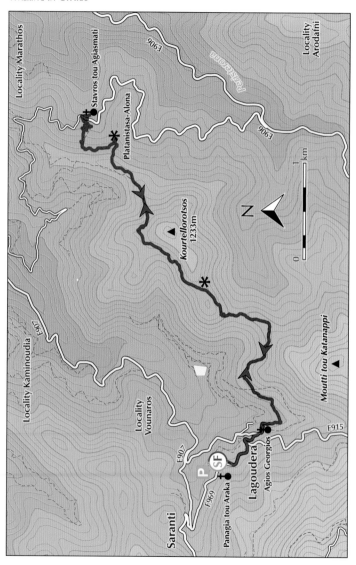

From Panagia tou Araka church, walk up the tarmac road to the village of **Lagoudera**. At the junction, go left towards Lefkosia. At the next intersection, carry straight on. (There is an E4 sign on a lamppost.) At the next junction keep left downhill, and shortly after that go right. Follow the nature trail sign straight on and a few minutes later pass Lagoudera's final house. Go downhill and soon cross a streambed. Pass by huge rocks and then the path crawls slightly uphill alongside vineyards and almond trees.

About 10–15min after passing the final house, cross a dirt track and continue uphill on its other side. ▶ Soon, rock roses and golden oaks replace the old vineyards and

On the left the view is dominated by the houses of Lagoudera nestled on the steep hillside with the peak of Madari towering above them.

The trail offers unrestricted views to the surrounding area

131

almond trees and a reservoir down below can be spotted. The stony path continues steadily uphill with magnificent views of the surrounding mountains, and about 20min after the first it meets another dirt track. Keep left and a few metres further on leave the dirt track to the left as the E4 sign indicates.

Pine trees are the main vegetation and mountains dominate the views as you walk along the stony path. Approximately halfway along the route you reach a **viewpoint** where the splendid vista of Cape Kormakitis/ Kormacit and Morfou Bay greets you. From this point, continue to walk mainly downhill for 40–50min to reach the next signposted viewpoint (**Platanistara-Aloua**). ◄ The narrow path runs beneath pine trees and from the Platanistara-Aloua viewpoint it bends to the left and soon runs between almond trees.

This part of the route is made more difficult by very steep downhill sections on occasionally loose surfaces.

The path splits and a wooden sign shows the two different routes: the steeper one is only 160m, while the other gently descends for 310m. Take either branch as the two paths soon rejoin just before emerging onto a dirt track. Keep left and then reach a junction where you go right and walk down to the **church**. ◄

There is a picnic table in the shade of trees and running water and toilets can also be found by the church.

The 15th-century UNESCO-listed church of **Stavros tou Agiasmati** remains slightly remote as it is situated 3km outside of Platanistasa village. It is home to the most complete 15th-century mural paintings in Cyprus. The church is closed but there is a phone number on the door to call if you haven't pre-arranged a visit and you want to see the interior.

After visiting the church, take a rest under the shade of trees and then retrace your steps to **Lagoudera**.

WALK 23
Politiko Nature Trail

Start/Finish	1km NE of Machairas Monastery (N34.94416, E33.19524)
Distance	12km (7½ miles)
Ascent/Descent	380m/380m
Grade	1
Time	4hr
Refreshments	Machairas Monastery
Access	On the E902 road, turn right just before Machairas Monastery and about 1km downhill a map board marks the beginning of the trail; there is space to park here.

This nature trail follows a quiet valley cut by the Pedieos river. The mighty building of the Machairas Monastery overlooks the valley as you start the trail. The path then undulates on the hillside following the lush riverbed. Like many other nature trails in this area, Politiko Nature Trail ends abruptly by a rural road, therefore you will need to retrace your steps.

MACHAIRAS MONASTERY

An icon of the Virgin Mary – believed to be painted by the Apostle Luke – was found in a local cave in 1145 by two hermits, Neophytos and Ignatius, who used a knife to cut through thick bushes to reach it. A church was founded on the site in 1172 and was later expanded into a monastery. The name 'Machairas' comes from the Greek word *makhaira*, which means knife. In 1530 and then in 1892, fire destroyed the monastery but the icon survived.

From the information board, walk downhill on the dirt track and a few minutes later, where the road bends right, join a narrow path which starts on the right, going slightly uphill. ▶ About 10min from the information board there is a small path leaving the trail to the right; it is a detour to an **EOKA hideout**.

The Pedieos riverbed splits the hills and the only building, a small church, can be spotted on the opposite side of the gorge.

133

The hideout where Grigoris Afxentiou was killed in 1957

During EOKA's fights in the 1950s, **Grigoris Afxentiou**, their second-in-command, went into hiding in the Machairas Monastery. He was trapped and killed by the British in a hideout nearby on 3 March 1957. You can take a short detour to the hideout, which is decorated with wreaths. Afxentiou is regarded by the Cypriots as a national hero and a statue of him stands on the mountain close to the monastery, clearly visible from the Politiko Nature Trail.

However, the trail continues straight on and soon crosses a wooden **bridge**. There is an olive tree plantation down in the valley next to the river, but soon pine trees, golden oaks and rock roses are the main vegetation.

The narrow path meanders among pine trees. Keep straight on when the sign indicates and ignore any paths joining in from the right. As the valley narrows you can see the stony riverbed, and about 1hr from the start – approximately halfway – you descend slightly to reach another wooden **bridge**. Cross over it and then continue on the other side of the valley with captivating views to the narrow gorge and the surrounding hills.

134

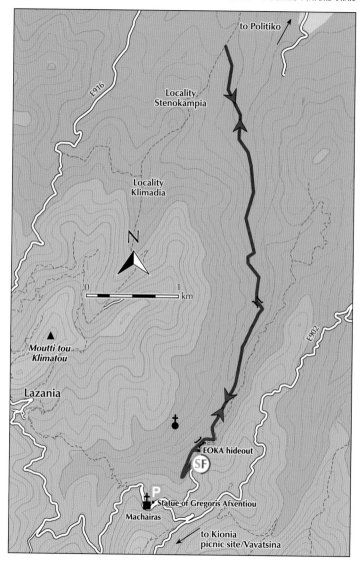

A rocky slope with pines on the top dominates the views on the right. The path curves around the mountainside and as the gorge widens again you'll see a dirt track and then some cultivated fields on the slopes on the other side of the valley. The path runs downhill and crosses a stream, then you walk uphill and swing away from the valley. Notice some buildings on the hill to the left and arrive at a dirt track by a fence. Follow this track by cultivated lands and a few minutes later arrive at a tarmac road and map board, where the nature trail ends abruptly.

There is not much to see from this point, so retrace your steps on the charming path back to the information board marking the beginning of the trail.

WALK 24

Machairas Monastery – Fikardou

Start	Machairas Monastery (N34.94158, E33.18909)
Alternative start	Kionia picnic site (N34.92091, E33.19771)
Finish	Fikardou
Distance	5km (3 miles); from Kionia picnic site: 10km (6¼ miles)
Ascent/Descent	310m/280m; from Kionia picnic site: 600m/980m
Grade	2
Time	2hr; from Kionia picnic site: 3hr 45min
Refreshments	Machairas Monastery, tavern in Lazania and restaurant in Fikardou
Access	From the A1 take the E105 towards Vavatsinia. Kionia picnic site (alternative start) is located about 8km north of Vavatsinia. For Machairas Monastery follow the road signs north from Kionia picnic site. Parking available at both.
Note	Starting from the Kionia picnic site adds an additional 1hr 45min (5km) to the walk. If you are planning to retrace your steps from Fikardou, allow plenty of time as there are some steep ascents along the way. Otherwise, transport from Fikardou should be arranged before the walk is started.

An E4-signed narrow path with excellent views to the mountains steeply descends from Machairas Monastery to a valley and then climbs to the tiny village of Lazania before continuing to the charming Fikardou village. Exploring the narrow streets of Fikardou feels like walking in the 18th century.

Starting from Kionia picnic site

Go up the steps between the picnic tables and arrive at the tarmac road that runs above the picnic site and leads up to the peak of Machairas with its radar dome. Turn right onto this road and follow it for about 600m to reach a **barrier**. An E4 sign with a map board on the right marks the start of the trail.

Leave the tarmac road to the right and walk uphill through a wooded area. The path passes the peak of Machairas with its dome towering at the top. Soon it gradually bends to the north and you walk along the ridge towards Machairas Monastery.

About 40min after leaving Kionia picnic site, start to zigzag downhill on the narrow stony path with views to pine-covered mountains as well as the snaking tarmac road below. Zigzag for 20–30min and emerge onto a dirt

The narrow path goes through a shallow valley with sparse vegetation

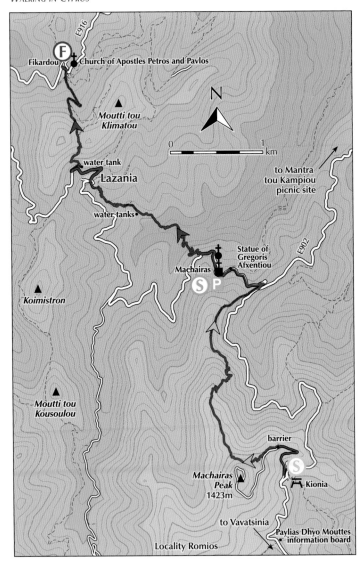

Fikardou

Church of Apostles Petros and Pavlos

Moutti tou Klimatou

water tank

Lazania

water tanks

Statue of Gregoris Afxentiou

Machairas

Koimistron

to Mantra tou Kampiou picnic site

Moutti tou Kousoulou

barrier

Kionia

Machairas Peak 1423m

to Vavatsinia

Locality Romios

Paylias Dhyo Mouttes information board

track. Keep right, and where another track joins in keep right again. About 10–15min after joining the dirt track you will reach a tarmac road junction; follow the tarmac road on the left towards **Machairas Monastery**, which you may opt to visit. From its car park continue on the tarmac road towards Lazania.

From the monastery car park, walk on the tarmac road towards Lazania. The path starts on the right, going steeply downhill from the road about 200m from the car park. (At the time of writing the E4 sign was missing but the narrow path was clearly visible.) Lazania's houses clinging to the opposite hillside draw your attention as you walk downhill between shrubs for about 15min and arrive at a streambed at the bottom of the valley.

Cross the stream over rocks and continue slightly uphill. Soon descend again by another streambed fringed by plane trees. The stony path levels out and runs along the edge of the mountainside, and shortly after the first it crosses a second streambed. Continue on the other side, zigzagging uphill between rock roses, occasional pines and olive trees. The vegetation is never too thick and you always have views of the mountains around you. ▶

On the left is the peak of Machairas in the distance.

Walk alongside a stone retaining wall and cultivated area and pass by two concrete **water tanks**. Continue to ascend and shortly arrive at a track. Keep left and a few metres further on an E4 sign marks the way uphill on a path to the right. There are some old olive trees by the path on your left and in front you Lazania's houses dominate the slope.

When you reach a dirt track, go right and it soon becomes a path again. Zigzag uphill and arrive at a road. Go left as the E4 sign shows and arrive in **Lazania** about an hour after leaving the monastery. Follow a narrow street between the old village houses and at the end of this narrow street turn right. Soon pass a small restaurant, and follow the tarmac road as the E4 sign indicates.

After leaving the village, ignore the first access road to the right. Leave the tarmac road on the second access road to the right, about 200m from Lazania's last house.

Go uphill on the stony track and just before reaching two water tanks, go left on a narrow path. Walk initially alongside a stone retaining wall with views to the roofs of Lazania's houses and the surrounding mountains.

Zigzag uphill between small shrubs and about 20min after leaving the tarmac road you will reach a gap between two hilltops. Start to descend towards Fikardou village with views towards the Kyrenia range and Morfou Bay. Pass a small house and a vineyard on the slope and continue to descend between golden oaks and other shrubs.

After a very steep downhill section you reach a concrete track; go left downhill. Soon it becomes a dirt track and as it swings around the mountainside the noises from the village can be heard. Arrive at a junction, keep right

The hills over Lazania are still recovering from a recent wildfire

140

and walk into the village. Arrive in **Fikardou** about an hour after leaving Lazania.

> **Fikardou** is a tiny picturesque village with narrow streets. Some houses have been restored to give insight into 18th-century village life. Two of the houses have been turned into a small museum. The village received the Europa Nostra Award in 1987 for its efforts in heritage conservation.

From Fikardou, if you haven't done so already, you may be able to arrange a taxi back to your start point. There are also a couple of daily buses to Nicosia. Alternatively you could retrace your steps, making a long and challenging day.

WALK 25
Kionia loop

Start/Finish	Paylias-Dhyo Mouttes trail head (N34.91420, E33.19630)
Alternative start/ finish	Kionia picnic site (N34.92091, E33.19771)
Distance	20km (12½ miles)
Ascent/Descent	1300m/1300m
Grade	3
Time	6hr
Refreshments	Fountain at Kionia picnic site
Access	From the A1 take the E105 road towards Vavatsinia. The information board for the Paylias-Dhyo Mouttes Nature Trail is located approximately 7km from Vavatsinia village on the right-hand side of the road. It is not easy to spot, but there is a dirt track on the opposite side of the road which may help to locate the starting point, where it is possible to park. Alternatively you can park at Kionia picnic site and start by walking back 1km (towards Vavatsinia) along the tarmac road to reach the Paylias-Dhyo Mouttes Nature Trail information board. Kionia picnic site is located about 8km from Vavatsinia.

The described walk, an out-and-back excursion, connects the short but spectacular Paylias-Dhyo Mouttes Nature Trail and the Kionia Nature Trail. The disued Profitis Elias monastery and the Kionia picnic site are connected by the Kionia Nature Trail, which runs as part of the E4 long-distance trail. Impressive views of unspoilt mountains as well as towards Nicosia and the North accompany you during this walk. There is only a very short section on tarmac road from the Kionia picnic site to the head of the Paylias-Dhyo Mouttes Nature Trail.

Walk uphill on the stony path with views towards the snaking tarmac road by the foot of Machairas peak. A few minutes after starting the trail, the path splits; keep right and walk uphill and instantly you are greeted by great views of the surrounding mountains.

The narrow stony path follows a small gorge for a while

At the next junction – about 900m from the information board – bear right on wooden steps and then continue uphill between golden oaks. As you climb higher – about 30min from the start – you reach a **viewpoint** sign. A short, narrow path takes you to the first peak of **Dhyo Mouttes** (1340m) where you can enjoy an almost

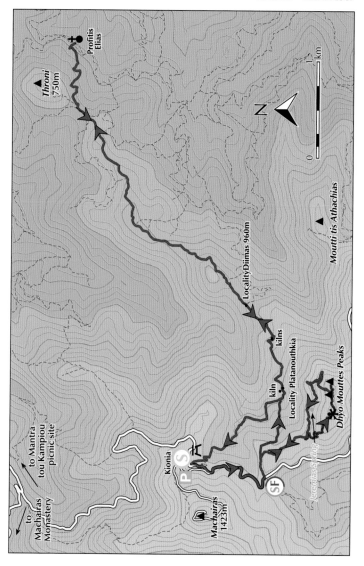

360-degree panorama. Admire the views and retrace your steps back to the path and continue to the left.

Descending slightly, look for the salt lake near Limassol in the distance. Shortly reach another **viewpoint** on the second peak of Dhyo Mouttes (1330m) just off the path on the right. ◀

From here you can easily recognise Machairas peak, Nicosia/Lefkoşa, the Kyrenia range and the first viewpoint.

Retrace your steps to the path. As you proceed downhill the Machairas peak is almost always visible. There are occasional steps as you zigzag downhill between golden oaks while continuing to enjoy excellent views towards Nicosia/Lefkoşa and the Kyrenia mountain range.

About 30min after the second viewpoint you arrive at **Jeramias spring** and shortly walk across deposits of talus rock and then pass by an old kiln. A few minutes after the spring you're back at the junction where you went uphill to the right; continue straight on and at the next intersection go right. Shortly pass by a small stone shelter, from where the path snakes steeply downhill. ◀

The vegetation is thick and the path is heavily eroded in places.

Less then a kilometre from the intersection, reach a clear path – the Kionia Nature Trail – and go right. Within a few minutes, pass **Locality Platanouthkia** and the site of a **kiln**, both marked with Greek signs only. Follow the

A beautiful view onto the rolling hills just before descending to Profitis Elias church

path downhill beneath pine trees and golden oaks, and just before reaching a dirt track pass by two big tar production **kilns**.

Reach a dirt road (**Locality Diimas**, 960m) and follow the E4 sign towards Profitis Elias. Soon walk along a ridge and as the path follows the contour of the mountain the view opens up towards Nicosia. Descend steadily and about 45min after the dirt road arrive at another dirt track where a sign indicates that Profitis Elias is 1km away.

Turn right off the road and continue downhill on the narrow path, which takes you to Profitis Elias picnic site (700m) and the abandoned **monastery**.

From Profitis Elias retrace your steps on the outward path for about 1hr 30min to the small junction where you joined the Kionia Trail, and then continue straight on. Follow the narrow path on the hillside, steadily uphill for about 40min with views dominated by unspoilt pine-covered mountains and rocks. Walk by a streambed and when the path splits, keep right and go uphill beneath mighty pine trees and a few minutes later arrive at the **Kionia picnic site**.

Climb up the stairs to the tarmac road; go left and walk about a kilometre on this road back to the start of the Paylias-Dhyo Mouttes Nature Trail.

WALK 26

Kakokefalos – Mantra tou Kampiou Trail

Start/Finish	Map board 1km north of Kionia picnic site (N34.927446, E33.201758)
Distance	12km (7½ miles)
Ascent/Descent	670m/670m
Grade	2 on the outward leg; 3 on the return
Time	4hr
Refreshments	Water fountain at Mantra tou Kampiou picnic site
Access	From Vavatsinia take the road north towards Machairas Monastery. Kionia picnic site is located in Machairas Forest about 8km from Vavatsinia village. From there, continue 1km north on the road towards Machairas to a picnic table with benches in a road bend. This is close to the starting point and there is space for parking.

This trail explores the Machairas Forest. Magnificent views towards the north accompany you as you walk steeply downhill on the often loose, stony path. From Mantra tou Kampiou there is a long dirt track heading onwards to Profitis Elias Monastery, but the walk described here takes you back on the same nature trail – therefore the return is a steep climb.

A map board marks the beginning of the trail. Leave the tarmac road via stone steps to the right. As you start the steep descent on the loose path, you almost immediately have views to the surrounding mountains. The path is eroded and loose because – as the many tyre marks suggest – it is used by mountain bikes as well as walkers. ◄

Mountain bikers shouldn't use the nature trails on the island as there are dedicated MTB routes, but you might see evidence suggesting otherwise.

The path swings steadily downhill with fine views towards Nicosia/Lefkoşa and the Kyrenia range. As you look back, the peak of Machairas with its radar dome stands out from the pine-covered mountains. After a steep descent of about 15–20min the path levels out

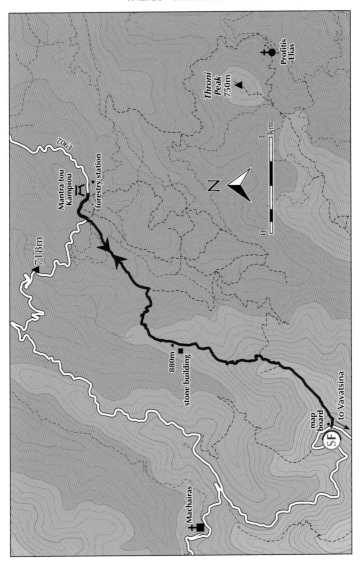

Profitis
Elias

Throni
Peak
750m

F902

Mantra tou
Kampiou

forestry station

718m

N

0   1 km

880m
stone building

map
board

SF

to Vavatsina

Machairas

147

View to the east from the ridge

The main vegetation, as is typical of this area, are pine trees, golden oaks and rock roses.

for a short while, and from the ridge you have more views. ◄

Continue, often on steep and loose surfaces, for a further 30–40min with excellent views to the mountains and towards Nicosia. After a long descent the path goes slightly uphill and arrives at a **stone hut** (at 880m) from where you can enjoy the panorama of the Mesaoria plains, the mountains and a network of dirt roads.

From the stone building, continue downhill and a few minutes later arrive at a junction. Ignore the wide track going uphill and keep right on the path as indicated by a white arrow on a wooden board. Zigzag downhill between pine trees for about 15min, and arriving at a dirt road go left. ◄

The streambed of Mantra tou Kampiou snakes along on the right.

Ignore any adjoining tracks and about 15min later reach a tarmac road. Go right, and a few minutes later arrive at the **Mantra tou Kampiou picnic site** where there are there are toilets, a water fountain, Machairas Forest information, a playground and plenty of picnic tables – a perfect place for a rest before the steep climb back to the start.

SOUTH AND EAST

Rolling hills near Kyparissia Peak (Walk 29)

Larnaca and Limassol, with their busy taverns and restaurants, are the two largest towns on the coast. However, you might prefer to take in the stunning views from the quiet hill near the Germasogeia Dam, only a few kilometres from bustling Limassol.

The UNESCO-listed Kourion Archaeological Site is only 13km from Limassol; from the ruins of its ancient acropolis you can admire the magnificent views of Episkopi Bay. Agia Napa is well known for its tourist resorts and nightlife, and the beaches in the area are popular with sun-lovers, but at nearby Cape Greco you might spend a quiet evening hunting for fossils.

A spectacular trail follows the rugged coastline near Pissouri, and you can visit Petra tou Romiou where according to legend Aphrodite rose from the sea. Not too far from the busy coast lies the peaceful Hapotami river gorge with the abandoned village of Kato Archimandrita.

The coastal towns cater amply for tourists with a wide range of accommodation, and you can easily take day trips to Machairas Forest or Troodos.

WALK 27

Hapotami Trail

Start/Finish	Kato Archimandrita church (N34.73673, E32.67993)
Distance	10km (6¼ miles)
Ascent/Descent	430m/430m
Grade	1
Time	3hr
Refreshments	None on route
Access	From Kouklia village take the F612 road towards Pano Archimandrita. Before reaching Pano Archimandrita leave the F612 to the right, signposted Kato Archimandrita. It is possible to park by the church opposite the only intact house in Kato Archimandrita.

Even though there are some well-kept plantations near the abandoned houses of Kato Archimandrita, it is a quiet place with a trickling stream meandering through the gorge. The often wide forest track follows the stream through the gorge and the water is crossed countless times. Leaving the stream behind, enjoy a bird's-eye view of the undisturbed sections of the deep gorge down below.

Kato Archimandrita, the lower part of the village of Archimandrita, was inhabited until 1962. However, its residents felt that the lack of school and suitable road to the upper part of the village isolated them, and they moved to Pano Archimandrita in 1962. Today the crumbling abandoned houses and an intact chapel dedicated to the Virgin Mary are what remains of the former village.

From the church, walk along the stony track between the ruins of houses. After about 5min arrive at a building with an arched gate and with an ancient olive tree in its yard. Turn left by this building and walk alongside a fenced plantation to the stream.

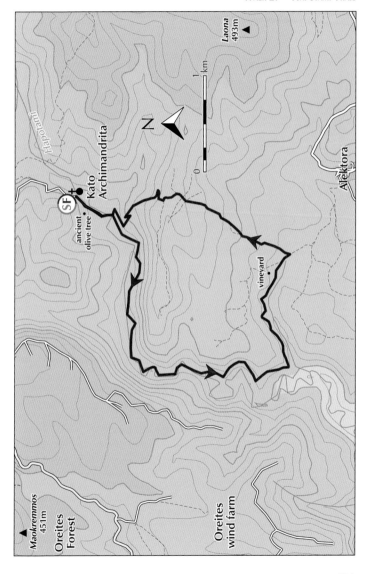

The remains of Kato Archimandrita

Cross the stream on slippery rocks for the first time and at the junction take the track on the right. As you walk beneath pine trees, wind turbines at the opposite side of the gorge soon come into view. The track follows the contour of the hillside and about 15–20min later reaches the stream again.

Over the next 45–55min you cross the stream numerous times on slippery rocks and often walk very close to it in the narrowing gorge. The track then bends slightly to the left and you start a gentle climb with the sight of the wind turbines on the top of the hills on the right. Walking by chalk walls, there is a mesmerizing view to the surrounding hills and to the winding narrow gorge down below. Then as the track swings to the left there's a bird's-eye view of the narrow, dense gorge.

Soon pass a **vineyard** and then some olive trees on the right. Carry straight on, ignoring other paths, and 5–8min after the vineyard reach a grey gravel road. Turn left towards the hill. As you walk gently uphill by young olive trees, the houses of the distant village of Alectora can be seen on the right.

The grey gravel road changes into a stony track lined with shrubs and rock roses and then levels out a bit. About 20–30min after joining the grey gravel road, the track divides; keep right and a few minutes later the track divides again. This time it is marked with cairns and you bear left.

Keep straight on at the next junction; soon there are remarkable views down to the Hapotami river gorge and the ruined houses of Kato Archimandrita. Go downhill, and follow the winding track back to the junction and the stream where you first crossed. Retrace your steps back to the **church**.

WALK 28
Pissouri coast walk

Start/Finish	Columbia Beach Resort, Pissouri (N34.64926, E32.71944)
Distance	11km (6¾ miles)
Ascent/Descent	640m/640m
Grade	3
Time	4hr
Refreshments	In Pissouri village, but none along the way
Access	Pissouri is located along the B6 road approximately halfway between Paphos/Baf and Limassol. There is a place to park near Columbia Beach Resort, close to the sea.

A there-and-back walk along an often crumbling narrow path along the coast with remarkable views to the rugged white limestone coastline. The turquoise sea crashes against the cliffs far below as you make your way along the overgrown trail towards a hidden pebble beach.

Extra care should be taken on the cliffs as the surface can be very loose in places. There is no shade and it can get very hot on a sunny day. Take plenty of water and sun protection.

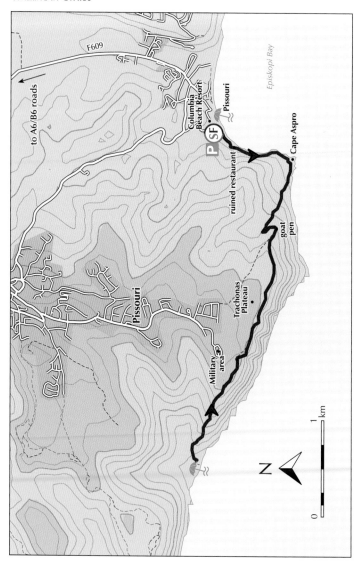

There are three different theories regarding the origin of the name **Pissouri**. The first is that it comes from the name of the ancient town of Voousoura. The second is that it derives from the Greek for 'very dark', as legend has it that the apostles met up in this area secretly at night. The third theory is that the name originates from the word *pissa* (resin), as that was the main product in this area during the Byzantine period. Today the scenic beach and the village on the hillside with its narrow streets attract many tourists.

Starting by the Columbia Beach Resort, walk towards the sea on a dirt track which bears slightly right. With the sea on your left, about 100m later arrive at the **ruins of a restaurant**. Go around the remains of the building on the gravel road, which then becomes a dirt road and ends about 50m later. The narrow, stony path starts on the edge of the cliff. Keep right, with the sea on your left, and soon arrive at an information board written in Greek only. ▶

Walk on the often eroded cliff-edge, occasionally marked with cairns. Soon descend on a loose, slippery surface towards a pebble beach (Cape Aspro). Cross a dry streambed and continue uphill on the rocky hillside on its other side. This is a steep section with interesting rock formations to look out for, and you might need to use your hands as you climb higher. ▶

There is a gorge on the right-hand side and you soon pass a few old olive trees. Continue on the narrow, eroded path and look out for stone cairns as they are the only signs – although they are not consistently placed along the route. The undergrowth becomes denser as you curve along the ledge of the gorge.

About an hour into the walk, reach a dirt track and keep left on the path, which becomes very overgrown as it reaches an old, ramshackle **goat pen**. Go around the fenced area on the cliff-edge, then go up on the ridge with the sea on your left, ignoring the track just after the pen.

Looking back, there are already great views of Pissouri Beach.

The slope is constantly exposed to erosion, therefore the path might alter.

155

View of the shoreline from the ridge path

Huge, white chalky cliffs towering above the sea fill the horizon and after about 8min of walking uphill on the ridge you reach the grassy **Trachonas Plateau**. Soon join a dirt track and follow it for about 130m. The scenery is interrupted by a military building with a radar and further in the distance by a telecommunications antenna. When the track bends right towards the **military building**, leave it and stay close to the sea. There is an overgrown, unclear path running along the edge and you are soon back on a dirt track where the wind turbines near the Hapotami gorge come into view.

There are cairns along the route but you might have to alter your way in some places.

As you walk along a ridge with views to the turquoise sea on the left and to a gorge and hills on the right, you'll soon see a long pebble beach. Shortly the path starts to descend. You can go all the way down to the beach but the ground is very loose and steep. You will also have to climb back along the very same path. ◄

The remote **beach** is a peaceful spot for a rest before retracing your steps to **Pissouri**.

WALK 29

Kyparissia Trail

Start/Finish	Germasogeia Dam car park, about 700m from Foinikaria village centre (N34.75632, E33.09616)
Distance	12km (7½ miles)
Ascent/Descent	750m/750m
Grade	2
Time	4hr
Refreshments	None on the way: take plenty of drinking water
Access	From the direction of Limassol, take the F128 road and turn towards Foinikaria. Pass a viewpoint, turn left on the next road (Frakti Street) and follow this to Germasogeia Dam car park.

Very close to lively Limassol, these pleasant paths lead up to Kyparissia's peak where you can enjoy views towards Limassol on the coast and the nearby Germasogeia Dam. The first part of the trail climbs steadily uphill with views to pine tree-dotted slopes. The walk includes the main section of the Kyparissia Nature Trail. There is very little shade on the hillside so it can get very hot on sunny days.

From the car park, walk on the tarmac road uphill for about 700m and then turn left towards Calabria. Go for a further 300m, where a green walker sign marks the start of the trail on the left. Follow the wide rocky track for about 10–15min with views towards the dam and Foinikaria village. Go left uphill on a dirt track as the walker sign indicates, and about 15min later leave it to the right when you see a green walker sign with an arrow.

Follow the winding, stony path uphill with views of the surrounding hills. Ahead is a small sharp peak and the dam is slightly behind you at this point. ▶ The path swings to the left and a steep towering hillside obstructs the view to the left for a few minutes. Shortly, the hill

The surrounding hillside is scattered with pine and olive trees.

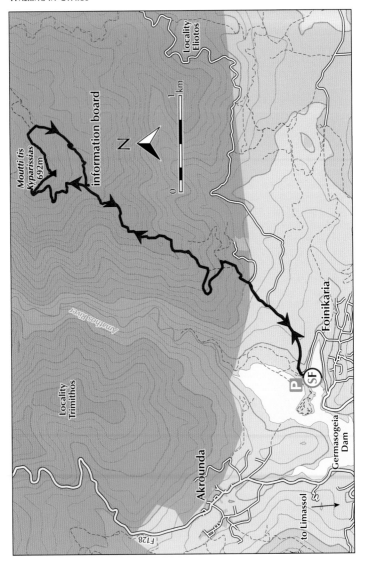

View from Moutti tis Kyparissias

gives way to fine views again towards the dam and Limassol on the far left.

Soon spot a roofed viewing platform in front of you at the top of the hill, then reach a small **information board** with a map of the nature trail. Here the path splits; keep left. (You will return from the hill on the other path.) The narrow, stony path climbs steadily with great views to the dam, Limassol, the salt lake and the coastline. ▸

About 15min after the path split, reach a dirt track. This junction is not signposted, but keep right and soon reach a sign: 'Kyparissia Peak 100m'. Turn right to make your final ascent to **Moutti tis Kyparissias** (692m).

Here you will see the familiar nature trail labels naming some of the bushes and trees.

On **Moutti tis Kyparissias** there is a roofed viewpoint that you may have seen earlier. Take a break on a bench and enjoy the excellent panorama towards Limassol and the coast. The mountain's name refers to the numerous cypress trees that populate it, especially on its higher sections.

Continue downhill on the wide track just behind the viewpoint. A few minutes later, at an unmarked

159

intersection, keep right and very soon reach another junction where you bear right, downhill. Shortly, at the next intersection, go right again as the green walker sign indicates. In front of you, between the crowns of trees, are views towards Limassol. ◄

As you descend, pines and junipers offer occasional shade.

About 30min after leaving Kyparissia's peak, reach and cross a streambed and continue on its other side. Walk with the streambed on your left and a few minutes later arrive back at the junction with the **map board** where the path split. Continue straight and retrace your steps back to the **car park**.

WALK 30

Sea caves – Kavos Hill

Start/Finish	Sea caves, Cape Greco/Poyraz Burnu (N34.96827, E34.05497)
Distance	6km (3¾ miles)
Ascent/Descent	165m/165m
Grade	1
Time	2hr
Refreshments	None
Access	Arriving from the direction of Agia Napa on the E306, turn off onto the E307 towards Cavo Greco Visitor Centre. The turn-off for the sea caves is on the right a few hundred metres from the road junction. Parking available.

Just a stone's throw from the busy beaches of Agia Napa lies Cape Greco National Park, a protected area and part of the Natura 2000 conservation project. The dramatic coastline washed by turquoise water is explored by boat by many holidaymakers. The trail described here is a popular one, and in particular the viewpoint on top of Kavos Hill is a favourite among visitors as it can be accessed from a nearby car park. From here you can enjoy the panorama of the rugged coast. Look out for fossils as you pass rocks along the trail.

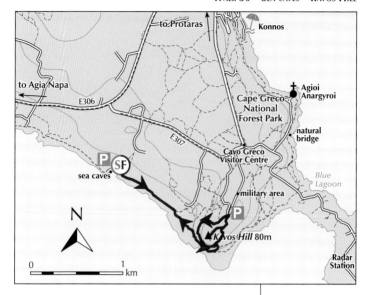

From the sea caves, walk with the sea on your right towards the rocky Kavos Hill. The well-trodden path runs parallel to the rugged shore on rocky ground, but it is easy to wander off as you enjoy the scenery. Nature trail signs and cairns help you stay on the right path.

About 15min after leaving the sea caves, cross a wide track and continue on its other side. From here there are E4 signs, and soon you join another track. Go right on this wide dusty track as the E4 sign indicates – it runs parallel to the sea with the sheer rock face of Kavos Hill towering on your left.

Stay on the path signed 'E4' and keep an eye out for a path that goes uphill on the left. Ascend on this narrow stony path. There are some faint trails on the hillside but stay on the well-trodden path snaking uphill, with views to the sea. Reach a dirt road, keep left and shortly arrive at a roofed viewpoint on top of **Kavos Hill**. ▶

Drink in the view and then go downhill on the dirt track that leads to a car park. Go left on the path marked

The near-white rugged coastline leads the eye all the way to Agia Napa.

The narrow, stony path before ascending to Kavos Hill

'Kavos Path'. As you walk slightly downhill, the rocky hillside dominates on your left. Soon reach a dirt track and turn left.

Continue on the track with Kavos Hill on your left and Agia Napa in the distance on the right. The path then curves around the hill. When it splits, keep going downhill. (The other path is the one you took to make your way to the top.) Walk all the way back to the dusty track (10–15min) and retrace your steps to the **sea caves**.

AGIA NAPA SEA MONSTER

Legend has it that a sea monster lives in the waters of Agia Napa. Fishermen call it *To Filiko Teras* (The Friendly Monster) as it never harmed humans, but was known to drag away fishing nets. Many believe that the sea monster is connected to Scylla, the sea creature from Greek mythology that appears on mosaics in the House of Dionysos in Paphos. Many tourists board boats in the hope of getting a glimpse of the legendary sea creature.

As you walk along the coastal paths of Capo Greco, you are more likely to see fossils of former creatures than the legendary sea monster.

WALK 31

Agioi Anargyroi – Cyclops Cave

Start/Finish	Agioi Anargyroi church (N34.97532, E34.07584)
Distance	6.5km (4 miles)
Ascent/Descent	165m/165m
Grade	1
Time	2hr
Refreshments	Café and restaurant at Konnos/Konnoi Beach
Access	Arriving from the direction of Agia Napa on the E306, turn right onto the E307 towards Cavo Greco Visitor Centre. Reaching the visitor centre, keep right towards Kamara toy Koraka (Natural Bridge) then turn left at the next junction to reach the Natural Bridge and Agioi Anargyroi church. There is a car park at the church.

Follow the rugged coastline with amazing views of lazily rocking boats on the turquoise sea. There is no shade on this trail so it can get really hot between May and October, but you can stop for a swim at Konnos Beach. This out-and-back trail is part of the E4.

The 'Konnoi – Agioi Anargyroi Path' sign marks the beginning of the trail near the church. Follow the narrow path, with the sea on your right, towards Konnos Beach, which

*Agioi Anargyroi
Church in the
distance*

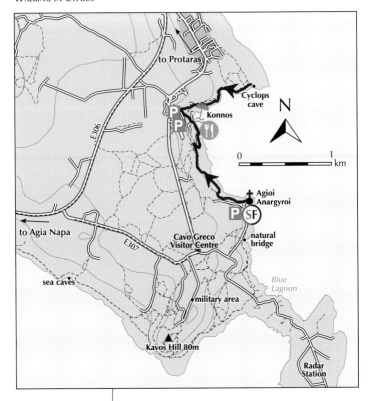

is visible from the church. Walk among trees and up on the steps. There are other paths in the bush, but always keep close to the sea if there isn't an E4 sign or an arrow to indicate direction.

Walk towards the beach and the hotel building on the slope. A few steps lead downhill; arrive at a path, go right as an arrow indicates and then the path swings to the left by the sea. About 30min after leaving the church, arrive at **Konnos Beach**.

Walk between the café's tables and then cross the car park. At the end of the car park there is a 'Konnoi

Konnos Beach from the opposite side of the bay

– Cyclops Cave Path' sign; follow the path on the barren slope with the beach on your right and a rocky wall on your left. When the path splits, keep right downhill, closer to the sea (the other path goes the same way but on the upper level). When the path splits again keep right, closer to the sea. ▶ Soon you will arrive at a rocky clearing where there is a viewpoint and steps leading down to the **cave**.

The path might be a bit eroded in places so take care.

After visiting the cave, walk back to Konnos Beach where you might want to stop for a swim before continuing to the church where you started the walk.

CYCLOPS

Cyclops is a giant, one-eyed, strong and wild creature of Greek mythology. The word *cyclops* means 'round- or circle-eyed'.

In Homer's *Odyssey*, when Odysseus arrived on the Island of Cyclops he found a cave and he and his men ate the food that was inside it. But the cave was home to Polyphemus, who was a cyclops. The cyclops returned to his cave in the evening and trapped Odysseus and his crew and ate some of the men. Odysseus hatched an escape plan: he gave Polyphemus some strong wine and then blinded him. When the cyclops, groaning in pain, asked who had attacked him, Odysseus told him: nobody. In the morning, as Polyphemus was letting his sheep out, he touched each animal's back to check if anyone was riding on them, but the men left the cave tied under the sheep's bellies.

According to cyclops stories, the creature had a link with blacksmithing, since blacksmiths covered one eye with an eye patch so that flying sparks wouldn't blind them in both eyes.

Another possible explanation of the cyclops legend was uncovered in 1914, when prehistoric dwarf elephant skulls were found on Cyprus, Crete, Malta and Sicily. The paleontologist Othenio Abel suggested that the central cavity in the skull might have been a large single eye-socket.

Cyclops Cave

NORTHERN CYPRUS

The route gets close to a vertical rock face near Karsiyaka village (Walk 33)

Mesaoria Plain, seen from near the Fourth Castle (Walk 35)

The Kyrenia mountains dominate the landscape of the northern part of the island. Winding trails snake up to castle ruins perched on rocks, where magnificent panoramas can be enjoyed. Pine-covered mountains fill the horizon and birdsong accompanies walkers on the trails. Kyrenia/Girne and the nearby villages on the coast offer a range of accommodation and serve visitors with shops and restaurants, making the area an ideal base for walkers.

A couple of miles from Kyrenia lies the small village of Bellapais, where the British author Lawrence Durrell lived from 1953–56. His book *Bitter Lemons of Cyprus* gives an insight of the everyday life of Cyprus in the 50s. There are marvellous views towards the coast from the impressive Bellapais Abbey, as well as small cafés for lazy afternoons.

The narrow Karpaz/Karpass Peninsula, like an outstretched arm pointing towards Turkey, attracts visitors with its long sandy beaches and wild donkeys.

The ruins of the ancient city of Salamis, near Famagusta/Gazimağusa, are well known and visited by tourist groups. Famagusta was an important trading port from medieval times; it is also known for the sad story of Varosha/Maraş. In the 60s and early 70s Varosha, a suburb of Famagusta, was home to glamorous hotels stretching along a long sandy beach. In August 1974 the Turkish Army invaded the town and Greek Cypriots left their homes and belongings in the hope that they could return after the conflict. However, this never happened as the Turkish Army fenced off Varosha, and since 1974 it has remained a ghost town.

WALK 32
Monumental olive trees of Kalkanli

Start/Finish	Picnic site by Cardac Café, between Tepebasi and Kalkanli villages (N35.26717, E33.04188)
Distance	8km (5 miles)
Ascent/Descent	90m/90m
Grade	1
Time	2hr 40min
Refreshments	Cardac Café
Access	Cardac Café is about 2km north of Kalkanli on the road to Tepebasi. Parking available near the café building.

The route starts at a picnic site and follows a small watercourse beneath trees to an ancient olive orchard. Wander between the olive trees and admire their venerable age before returning to the start on dirt tracks.

Facing the information board in front of the café, go left downhill as the green/white trail signs indicate. The trail gate is located by a spring. The path starts amid lush vegetation and follows the watercourse. ▶

At a junction, take the middle track slightly uphill and a few metres later leave this track on a path to the right. There are green signs marking this section of the trail. Eucalyptus trees grow by the path, which runs parallel to a dirt track with a wide valley on the right.

Reach a dirt track, cross it diagonally and continue on its other side downhill to arrive back alongside the watercourse. A few metres later go left uphill as the sign on a tree indicates. When the path splits, keep left and pass a small **stone ruin**. Shortly afterwards arrive at a dirt track, turn right and a few metres later leave it to the left, going slightly downhill.

Follow the green signs, accompanied by the sound of gurgling water and a concert of frogs. Ignore a path

The water disappears into a pipe for a while just after the picnic site.

Ancient olive trees

The fence protects the olive trees from goats.

The reservoir holds springwater for the orchard.

joining from the right; keep straight, cross a small wooden bridge and then continue next to the watercourse. The path might not be clearly visible, but stay next to the watercourse and about 20min after the wooden bridge arrive at a fenced area. ◄

Open the gate and follow the watercourse into the olive orchard. About 50m from the gate go left and join a dirt track close to the water channel. Pass a bench and continue along a path. Arrive at an information board near a **reservoir**. ◄ Take time to wander among the ancient **olive trees**.

The **Monumental Olive Trees** were planted during the 1200s. The oldest tree is over 800 years old and about 400 of the trees are over 500 years old. It is a protected area.

To leave the orchard, find the dirt track in the middle (you can walk down on this dirt track from the information board near the reservoir), follow it towards the buildings on the top of a mountain and leave the fenced area via a big **gate**. Follow the dirt track curving right by the

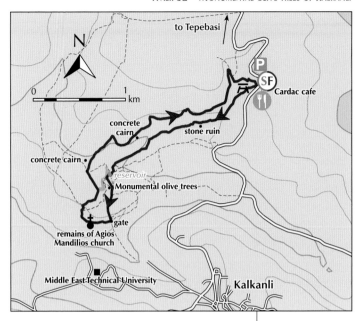

fenced area (there are some green circle signs here) with a valley on your left and some eucalyptus trees near the streambed.

Pass the spot where the **Agios Mandilios church** once stood and continue along the fence. Turn right by the fence, uphill, and a few minutes later leave the fence behind and continue on the dirt track as it bends to the left. About 150m later, at a junction, take the second track from the right. Pass a **concrete cairn** as you follow the dirt track. Ignore a track on the left, and pass another **concrete cairn**.

Ignore any tracks on both sides and about 30–40min after leaving the fence, arrive back at the roadside café with the picnic site. When you see the building the track curves right; reach the picnic benches and walk up to the building and information board.

WALK 33
Sina Monastery circular

Start/Finish	Karsiyaka Mosque, Karsiyaka village (N35.34439, E33.12374)
Distance	5km (3 miles)
Ascent/Descent	290m/290m
Grade	1
Time	1hr 45min
Refreshments	Bar in Karsiyaka village
Access	Leave the Coastal Road for Karsiyaka village. In the village find the mosque with a car park next to it (the minaret is visible).

The ruins of the monastery sit on the hillside above the village, overlooking the sea. Wander around between the old walls and then climb up to a small rocky peak where you can enjoy the magnificent panorama. The second section of the trail is a descent on a steep hillside and the last short section is on tarmac road.

From the mosque, walk west on the tarmac road, ignore the road on the left just after the mosque and continue west until you reach Monestir Sokak, where the trail starts. A few metres later it becomes a dirt track. Follow this track – ignoring any joining tracks – to the **ruins of Sina Monastery**.

The once-grand **Sina Monastery** sits on the hillside with towering mountains in the background. There is very little information available about this monastery, but the ruins suggest it was an important building and was rebuilt many times before being abandoned.

When Lord Kitchener did a survey of Cyprus in 1882, the monastery was already in ruins. You can

Sina Monastery and Karsiyaka beyond

wander around the site and enjoy the great views towards the coast.

Continue uphill on the same dirt track and turn right by a water pipe. Soon spot a green 'B' sign on a rock; from here this will mark the trail. The narrow path snakes between bushes towards the rocky mountain and you are soon accompanied by magnificent views of the monastery, the village and the coast.

Climb up some stone steps and then zigzag uphill on the narrow path by a huge rock wall with great views towards the coast. Sina Monastery is slightly behind you on your right as you ascend. Reach the large rocks near a small **peak** about 30min after leaving the ruins. Take a last glimpse of the monastery. From the rocks, the rugged coastline leads the eye to the distance where the sea and the sky meet.

The path goes around the large rock and bends left downhill. Zigzag downhill for about 15min with views towards the coastline and mountains. ▶ After some stone steps, arrive at a half-tarmac half-dirt track. Go right on this wide track, cross a **stone bridge**, and a few minutes

There are some steep sections and the surface can be loose and slippery in places.

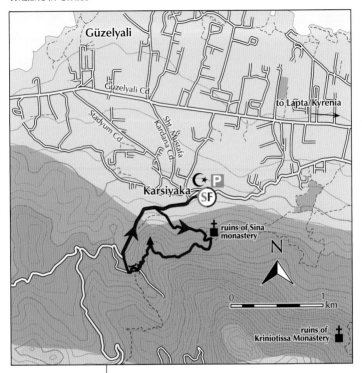

later notice a rough dirt track going steeply downhill on the right. Go down this rough track to reach the tarmac road (or you can follow the dirt track all the way to the tarmac road). When you arrive at the tarmac road, go right and follow it for about 15min back to **Karsiyaka**.

WALK 34

Lapta Baspinar Trail

Start/Finish	Baspinar old spring, SW corner of Lapithos/Lapta (N35.33135 E33.16844)
Distance	12km (7½ miles)
Ascent/Descent	830m/830m
Grade	3
Time	5hr 30min
Refreshments	None on the way
Access	Leave the Coastal Road for Lapithos/Lapta and follow the narrow, winding road uphill to the Baspinar spring. The use of GPS coordinates for the start is highly recommended because of the complicated network of streets of the village. There is place to park near the spring.

The first challenge is to find the beginning of the trail. Winding narrow roads take you between Lapta's houses – clinging on the steep mountainside – to the trail gate. There are some sections where the path is hardly visible and route-finding can be a challenge, but there are different-coloured paint marks on rocks to look out for. The first half of the trail runs steeply uphill with magnificent views. On the descent you will find the ruins of a small monastery hidden by trees. The return to Lapta follows dirt tracks with grand views towards the coast.

There is an information board near the Baspinar old spring. From here, go right along the dirt track with a retaining wall on your left. After passing a building, views open up towards the coast on the right. When the track splits, keep left uphill as the green/white 'B' sign indicates, and at the junction go left uphill and arrive at the Lapta–Baspinar Parkuru **trail gate**. The narrow path – marked with red paint on rock – starts steeply uphill by the trail gate.

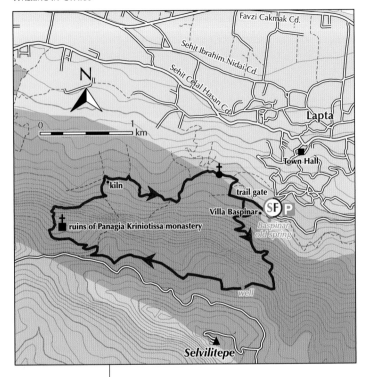

As you follow the stony path zigzagging uphill towards the rocky mountains, you will spot faint red arrows on the rocks. Enjoy some fine views towards the coast as you ascend by boulders on the cypress-scattered slope. About 20min after joining the narrow path, arrive at a sheer rock wall with an arrow pointing both ways. Go left.

Follow the path and then continue to zigzag uphill, passing rock walls and boulders. ◄ As you ascend on the shrub-, pine- and cypress-scattered rocky mountainside there are splendid views of Lapta and the coast.

Occasional paint marks on rocks indicate the right direction.

Ascend through forest, and about 1hr 15min after passing the sheer rock wall with the arrows, the path

An exposed section of the trail

levels out and you'll see electricity poles on the nearby mountain. After a rocky section the path starts to descend; there are giant Calabrian pines nearby and soon some **ruins** on your right. (The path might be a bit overgrown here so look out for the painted red signs.)

Go through a wooded area, pass a stone trough and a deep **well**, and you'll see the remains of a stone wall. ▶ After this keep slightly right. Look out for the faint red and blue marks on rocks as the path is overgrown and might be difficult to spot. It leaves the forest and curves first right and then left and soon starts to descend. Again, look out for the faint paint marks as the path is not always

It's likely this area was once used to keep animals.

177

clearly visible. Follow the marked path downhill with some views to pine-dotted rocky mountains.

The path then curves right. Follow the contour of the mountainside with views to the mountains and the sea. Pass a retaining wall on your left and walk through a forest. About 50min after starting the descent, arrive at a wide track. Go left and slightly uphill and follow the track through the forest. ◄

Soon you have beautiful views to the sea, and in front of you the scene is dominated by a rocky mountain.

About 15min after joining the track, arrive at a junction; go right downhill, and at the next junction keep left as the red arrow indicates. Zigzag downhill along the forest track with views towards the coast. Ignore a track joining from the left and continue straight on downhill. The track becomes a narrow path; there is a pipeline on the path and then you go steeply downhill on loose steps. Pass a goat pen and arrive at the ruins of the **Panagia Kriniotissa monastery** hidden in semi-darkness in the shade of trees.

Ruins of Panagia Kriniotissa Monastery

Like a mysterious building from the pages of an old book, the roof of **Panagia Kriniotissa Monastery** is overgrown with grass and the walls are crumbling

down. Very little information can be found about the ruins. The monastery was most probably founded in the 12th century but was abandoned by 1735.

Turn left by the monastery and zigzag downhill as the red signs indicate. The path is not always clearly visible. Walk along the loose rocky path, which bends to the right and goes steeply downhill. About 30min after leaving the monastery, pass a rock wall. The path is overgrown but there are some green arrows indicating the direction.

As you descend among big boulders the path is not always clear and you really have to look out for faint paint marks on rocks. Follow the signs, ignoring a very steep path on the left. As you follow the contour of the mountain you can enjoy some impressive views towards the coast. Arrive at a dirt track, turn left and follow it downhill. For the next hour you will be following this dirt track, marked with green 'B' signs.

Pass a big **kiln** by the track. At a junction, turn right downhill as the green 'B' sign indicates, with an old retaining wall on the right. At the next intersection go right with views towards Lapta and the coast on the left. Ignore two consecutive tracks on the right, keeping straight on both times. ▶ Ignore a path on the left and continue slightly uphill as indicated by the green 'B' sign. Soon two flag masts dominate the hillside on your left. Ignore a track going downhill on the left.

Pass a derelict graveyard with the ruins of a **chapel**. When the track splits, go right as the green 'B' sign indicates. Pass the ruin of a small building and continue straight on as indicated. At the junction, go left and follow the dirt track straight back to the trail gate and then the **Baspinar old spring**.

Young pines grow by the track.

WALK 35

The Fourth Castle

Start/Finish	Agirdag village (N35.29802 E33.26640)
Distance	9.5km (6 miles)
Ascent/Descent	500m/500m
Grade	2
Time	3hr 30min
Refreshments	None: take plenty of water
Access	From the mosque in Agirdag (look for the minaret), take the street to the north and then fork left and at the next junction go left. Soon reach the beginning of the dirt track. Parking available.

The Fourth Castle may be dwarfed by its more popular neighbour, St Hilarion Castle (Walk 36), but its site is well worth a visit, and impressive views towards the south accompany you as you walk along the rocky mountainside towards it. As the ruins are in a somewhat remote location you will have to retrace your steps to Agirdag.

As you follow the track on the carob tree-scattered mountainside you can enjoy views towards Nicosia and the Troodos range.

The dirt track starts at the end of Agirda village and runs parallel to the mountain range. Pass a **goat pen** and soon notice a yellow arrow on a rock. ◄ Ignore two faint paths very close to each other on the right, and continue on the wide track, slightly uphill, between cypress and pines. Spot some red paint marks on the rocks.

The track bends slightly away from the mountains but soon curves towards them again. About 15min after leaving the village, notice some **beehives** on the left and ignore the track running towards them. After the beehives there is a small building on the left; ignore faint tracks first on the left and then on the right and continue on the

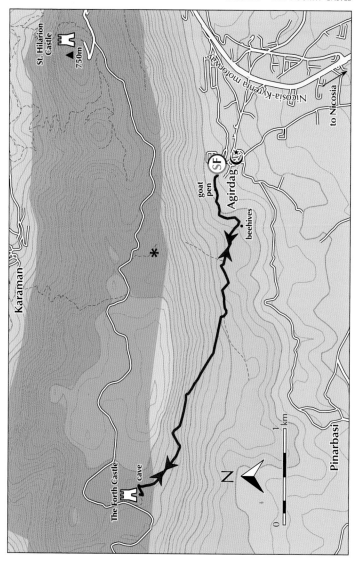

On the rock-scattered slope close to the foot of the towering mountain you might notice the ruins of a building with an old retaining wall.

wide track marked with some yellow, blue and red paint marks on rocks. ◄

As you approach the rock face there is a small ravine on your left, and you might catch sight of the contour of the peak of Machairas in the distance. Passing under an electricity wire, ignore the faint track on your left and then continue slightly uphill towards the rocky mountains. Shortly after the electricity wire there is a faint path on the left but continue straight on. (There are yellow arrows on rocks to help you identify the trail.) Trees grow closer to the dirt track here.

After a stony uphill section, arrive at a junction. Go right; there might be a cairn and red paint mark to indicate the direction. Soon there is a flat, grassy area on the right. Continue straight on uphill on the stony path as the yellow and red paint mark indicates. The rough track eventually becomes a narrow path and runs on the rocky mountainside with the towering mountain on your right and with great views towards the Troodos.

Unrestricted views from the rocky mountainside all the way to the castle

Follow this rocky path, mainly uphill, for about an hour. Vegetation is sparse; the mountainside is scattered with rock roses, thorny gorse and some olive trees. As

you walk close to a rock wall, enjoy the stunning views towards Morfou Bay. There are some cairns to help you to identify the path, which is clearly visible most of the time as you zigzag uphill.

Soon you have undisturbed, excellent views on the left, and the ruins of the Fourth Castle appear in front of you. A very short section of the path is slightly overgrown but it is still possible to follow it. Pass by a small '**cave**' and then the path bends left towards the ruins. Climb up to the remains of the **castle** before the track starts going downhill.

> Travel guides don't mention this **hidden ruin** as it is considerably smaller than the other three castles in the Kyrenia range and there is very little known about it. It was built around the same time as the other castles and was most probably used as a signal tower.

After visiting the ruins, retrace your steps to **Agirdag**.

WALK 36
St Hilarion Castle

Start/Finish	Cosku Sokak (street), Zeytinlik village (N35.32653, E33.29417)
Distance	11.5km (7 miles)
Ascent/Descent	760m/760m
Grade	3
Time	5hr (+ allow 1hr 30min to visit the castle)
Refreshments	Café at the entrance to St Hilarion Castle
Access	Cosku Sokak is on the south side of Girne Cevreyolu (road) in Zeytinlik. It is best to use the GPS coordinates given to find the start of the trail. There are plenty of places to park near the modern white buildings and the trail is easily accessible.

St Hilarion Castle – built hundreds of years ago and now in ruins – is perched on the rocks and still strictly looks over the sea and the mountains. As you wander around among the ruins and enjoy the panorama on a clear day, you can see why until the 10th century the castle played an important role in protecting the island from Arab attacks. The first and last sections of the trail follow dirt tracks with fine views. There is a climb on a narrow path towards the castle and a short section runs through a scenic gorge. The trail is waymarked, but you have to watch out for signs as they are inconsistent.

At Cosku Sokak, notice the green sign on a lamppost and leave the tarmac road just after the sign to the left. Follow this dirt track towards the mountains and a few minutes later, when it splits, keep right. Soon another dirt track joins from the left, but keep right as the green sign on a small rock on the ground indicates.

Arrive at a large, half-finished building and an asphalt road. Go left and uphill on this road towards the mountains. Walk by a fence and soon the asphalt road changes back to a dirt track. Keep straight on after the fence, and look for signs on the rocks as you follow this rock rose-lined track, with a gorge on your left.

This dirt track winds uphill with views towards Kyrenia/Girne and the sea for about 30min and arrives at a junction near an electricity pole. Turn right as the sign indicates. Soon a mixture of junipers and pines are the main vegetation alongside the track. About 10min after the electric pole, arrive at another dirt track near a building and keep right. (The left side of the dirt track is a forbidden area.)

Pass a **concrete water tank**; the track then goes slightly downhill and bends to the right. Another track joins from the right but keep straight on, looking for a green sign on a rock. As the dirt track crawls uphill it approaches the rocks. Pass another **water tank** and notice a track joining from the left from the forbidden area, so keep right towards the castle as the sign indicates. ◄

There are bushes around the track and rocks towering on your left.

As the dirt track curves, enjoy the views to Kyrenia and the coast on your right. At the dirt road junction, bear

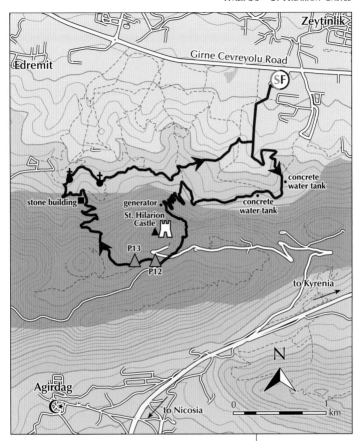

left and follow the stony track uphill. There are signs on rocks as you continue to ascend. Arrive at a **power generator** 1hr 10min after the junction with the electricity pole. A narrow path – marked with green signs – starts on the rocks by the building.

Ascend the steep rocky slope for 30–35min. Soon climb towards the tower and the **castle** wall, but just before reaching it, meet a grassy path, turn left and a few

minutes later arrive at a parking area. The trail continues on the other side of the tarmac road, marked with a
'Kocan Rest 20km' sign, but to visit the castle, take the
tarmac road on the right uphill.

ST HILARION CASTLE

The southern section of St Hilarion Castle

Along with the
Buffavento and Kantara
castles (Walks 37 and
43), St Hilarion Castle
was built to protect the
island from Arab attacks
between the seventh
and 10th centuries. St
Hilarion, from whom
the castle takes its name,
was a monk who lived
and died nearby. In the
10th century a church and a monastery were built and in the 11th century
fortification begun by the Byzantines. During the Lusignan period the castle
was rebuilt and might also have been used as a summer residence.

The ruins, nestled on high rocks, are said to be the inspiration for the
castle in the Walt Disney production *Snow White and the Seven Dwarfs*.

For a small entrance fee you can visit the ruins. Allow at least 1hr–1hr
30min to walk around and enjoy the views. Visiting hours: Apr–Oct, 9am–
5pm; Nov–Mar, 9am–2pm.

From the castle, retrace your steps to the car park
and continue on the tarmac road marked with the
'Kocan Rest 20km' sign. (Coming from the castle it is
on the right.)

Soon note a green sign painted on the tarmac road.
About 50m later, reach a **P12 pyramid** (T45 trail). Leave
the tarmac road to the right, on the dirt track going downhill by the pyramid. At the next pyramid (**P13**) bear right
on a narrow path which goes downhill and bends right
towards the coast. Look for green signs on rocks and soon
walk through a small gorge.

You only spend about 10min in the scenic gorge and then the path bends left, away from it. Leave the gorge and then continue to descend steeply on a stony path. There are the familiar green 'B' signs, but you will also see red arrows.

St Hilarion Castle – with its camouflaged top – in the distance

About 10min after leaving the gorge, arrive at a dirt track. Keep left and follow it downhill. ▶ On your right the castle sits high up on the top of the rocks. Pass the ruins of a **stone building**, and when another track joins keep left as the arrow indicates.

There are signs on the rocks by the track to help.

About 1hr 20min after leaving the castle, arrive at a junction. Go right and soon pass the ruins of a **chapel**. There is a gorge on your left as you continue, and when a dirt track joins from the left keep slightly uphill to the right. About 7min after the first, pass the ruins of a second **chapel**. A few metres after the second chapel, at a junction, go left downhill.

Continue to descend on the wide stony track with excellent views towards the coastline. There are green signs on the rocks by the track and when a track joins from left, keep straight on as the sign indicates.

Arrive at a clearing with views to Kyrenia, keep right, pass by a small fenced area and just after that a steep dirt track starts on the left. Follow this steep track and about 5min later arrive at an electricity pole with a green sign on it. Go sharply right and steeply downhill.

Emerge onto a dirt track by beehives an hour or so after you passed the ruins of the first chapel. Go left (the track on the right is where you went uphill towards the castle) and retrace your steps to the beginning of the trail.

WALK 37

Buffavento Castle

Start/Finish	Besparmak Buffavento restaurant (N35.27998, E33.46688)
Distance	18.5km (11½ miles)
Ascent/Descent	1150m/1150m
Grade	3
Time	7hr (+ allow 1hr to visit Buffavento Castle)
Refreshments	Besparmak Buffavento restaurant
Access	The restaurant is located by the Besparmac Caddesi road between Kyrenia/Girne and Nicosia/Lefkoşa. Parking available at restaurant or opposite building at beginning of trail.

The first part of this long but well-marked trail takes you on rock rose-covered mountainside with stunning views. There is an opportunity to visit the ruins of Buffavento Castle, from whose highest point you can enjoy a grand panorama. Wandering in the castle's ruins, it's easy to see why this was a good defensive position. A good section of the return route is on dirt tracks, but marvellous views accompany you along the way.

The trail starts opposite the Buffavento restaurant on the tarmac road, signed 'Buffavento Castle 6km'. Look for the first green 'B' sign on an electricity pole a few metres uphill and leave the tarmac road to the right on a narrow path. There are immediate views to Besparmak

Mountain, the snaking road, and soon towards the coast on your right.

Besparmak Mountain

BESPARMAK MOUNTAIN

Besparmak Mountain is also called the 'five-finger mountain' because of its shape. According to local legend, there was once a beautiful girl who lived in a village near the mountain. Two young men wanted to win her heart; they decided to have a duel on the edge of a marsh in Mesaoria. One of the men had an evil plan to win the duel and he pulled the other man into a marsh. As he was sinking, the young man held his sword above his head, the weapon slipped from his gasp and he sank with five fingers reaching towards the sky. When the marsh dried out the young man's hand became the mountain.

The hillside is scattered with white rocks and green rock roses. The stony path follows the contour of the mountain, and as you slowly leave the Besparmak Mountain behind, there are more views towards the coast. ▶ The view in front of you is dominated by a mountain scattered with white rocks and covered with rock roses.

Numerous green 'B' signs mark the clearly visible path.

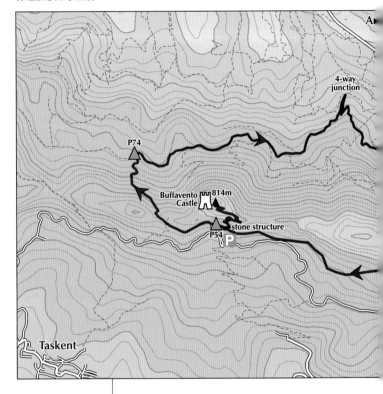

About 30min after starting from the restaurant, at a junction go left and slightly uphill as the green 'B' sign indicates. Soon you will get close to the road, but just before reaching it keep right as the green 'B' suggests. Follow this narrow path uphill between rock roses and rocks with views to the coast on your right.

Climb between boulders and soon the path levels out. Continue towards a rocky mountain with views on your left towards Nicosia/Lefkoşa and the Troodos mountains, and to the coastline on the right. As you descend towards the rocky mountain there are a few small pines but the main vegetation is still rock roses.

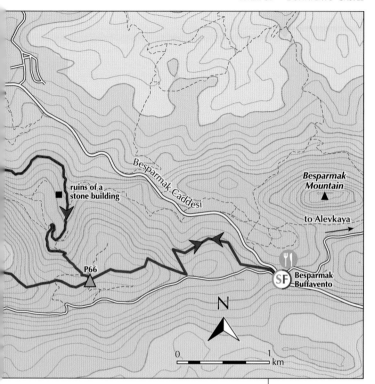

Reach a dirt track, cross it and continue on its other side by the **P66 pyramid**. (There is a green 'B' sign as well.) Follow the signs; the clearly visible path is well-marked and easy to follow. About 10min after the P66 pyramid there is a faint path on the right, but follow the green 'B' signs as the path bends left. Continue on the marked path, mainly uphill, with some views. About 40min after the P66 pyramid, start to descend. ▶

Soon pass a **stone building**; enjoy the excellent views towards the south. Follow the undulating path towards the ruins of the castle. Not long before reaching the car park, note the snaking tarmac road on the hillside. There

Soon you will get a first glimpse of Buffavento Castle perched on the rocks in the distance.

are some old retaining walls and olive and carob trees, suggesting that the hillside here might have once been cultivated.

About 40–45min after you caught the first glimpse of the ruins, arrive at a **car park**. Next to the information board a steep path with steps climbs up to the **castle**. Allow at least 20–30min to reach the top.

BUFFAVENTO CASTLE

The name of the castle means 'defier of the winds' or 'buffeted by winds'. The castle was most probably built as a watchtower in the first instance and then became a castle during the Lusignan period. With Kantara and St Hilarion castles (Walks 43 and 36) it formed part of a line of defence against Arab raids. As Buffavento was built higher up, signals could be sent to the other two castles. It also guarded an important pass through the mountains.

A magnificent 360-degree panorama can be enjoyed from the highest part of the castle. The ridge of the Kyrenia mountain range stretches into the endless distance. You should allow at least an hour to visit the castle, which includes the steep climb to the ruins.

The trail continues from the car park by the **P54 pyramid** (T6 trail) next to the steps. Pass the remains of a circular stone structure and walk with the towering rocks on your right and with views on your left.

About 10min after leaving the car park, a big Turkish Cypriot flag comes into view on the slope in front of you. There is a network of goat tracks on the hillside, but the trail is marked with green 'B' signs. ◄

Like a pile of Lego bricks, boulders scatter the hillside as you progress.

At a clearing, continue to ascend on a wider path and when it ends, turn sharply to the right and uphill as a big red arrow indicates. Soon there are pines by the path and you start to descend through a forest (there are some red and yellow marks along with the green 'B' signs). Ignore a faint path on the left and keep right as the green 'B' sign indicates, downhill. A few minutes later, ignore the unmarked path on the right and continue to the left downhill as the red arrow suggests.

There are strawberry trees as you descend through the forest, as well as some views on the right towards the coast. The path might be slightly overgrown here. Zigzag steeply downhill with great views to the coast. When you reach a wider path, go right downhill and soon it changes into a rough dirt track. ▶

About an hour after leaving the castle car park, arrive at a dirt track with a **P74 pyramid**. Go right (T49) on the dirt track. There are views to the coast on your left, pines line the dirt track and you may notice an old retaining wall on your right. At a junction, continue straight uphill (there is a green sign on a nearby tree) and a few minutes later at the next junction continue straight on, slightly downhill, as the green/white sign indicates. The dirt track follows the contour of the mountainside with views towards the coast on your left.

Ignore two consecutive tracks joining from the right and keep straight on both times. Fine views to the left accompany you most of the time and about 45min after joining the dirt track by the P74 pyramid, arrive at a **four-way junction**. Go sharply right, steeply uphill and spot a green sign on a concrete cube by the track. After a very steep section, the dirt track descends slightly and Besparmak Mountain comes into view.

Ignore the track that goes steeply uphill on the right, carry straight on – slightly downhill – and soon note a green sign on a rock. At the T-junction keep right as the green sign indicates. ▶

Soon the track levels out and you pass the **ruins of a stone building**. Ignore the path joining from the right as you walk beneath huge pines. About 50min after the four-way junction, arrive at a junction with a 'lighting of fire forbidden' sign and go right as the green sign indicates. Follow the wide track through a valley, slightly uphill, with a riverbed on your left.

The track bends away from the valley. At a junction bear left uphill on the white stony track, and a few metres later look out for a green sign on a rock. The track seems less used here, as it is overgrown by rock roses.

Buffavento Castle stands perched proudly high on the rocks on your right.

There are pines by the track on the right and views towards the coast on the left.

Stunning view to the north on the descent route

Very soon arrive at a junction with a 'P66' sign pointing to the right, and continue slightly uphill on the overgrown track. Reach a dirt track, turn left, and at the next junction bear right and arrive at the **P66 pyramid**. Turn left and retrace your steps, following the green 'B' signs to the **Buffavento restaurant**. It will take about 1hr to reach the restaurant from the P66 pyramid.

WALK 38

Armenian monastery

Start/Finish	Alevkaya picnic site (N35.28606; E33.53278)
Distance	9km (5½ miles)
Ascent/Descent	430m/430m
Grade	2
Time	3hr 30min–4hr
Refreshments	Café and water fountain at Alevkaya picnic site
Access	From Besparmak Buffavento restaurant on the Besparmak Caddesi road between Kyrenia/Girne and Nicosia/Lefkoşa, take the narrow winding tarmac road 9km to Alevkaya. The picnic site is obvious and there is space for parking.

Families gather together on Sundays at the popular picnic site in Alevkaya and the smell of burning wood and grilled meat drifts into the woods. However, Alevkaya and the forest are very quiet on weekday mornings. In the springtime the forest is home to orchids.

This route follows a narrow path on rock rose-covered hillsides with some great views. There is the opportunity to stop by the ruins of a church and then wander around the courtyard of the abandoned Sourp Magar Armenian monastery before returning to Alevkaya. Most of the trail is marked with green/white signs.

At **Alevkaya** there is a forest station, a herbarium, and plenty of places to park. There is also a café, a playground and lots of picnic tables in the shade of mighty trees.

From the information board, take the steps down and walk across the picnic area, passing a water fountain. The Alevkaya Kuzgun Parkuru trail gate is located at the end of the picnic area.

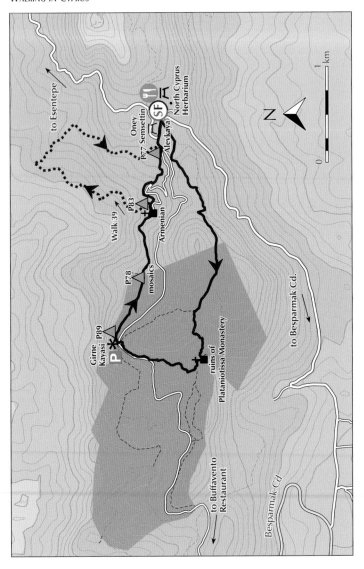

The narrow path starts between bushes, with rocks on the right. There are some steps downhill; where the path splits, keep left. A few minutes after the trail gate, reach a dirt track beneath pine trees; go right and very shortly at the junction bear left. Leave this dirt track to the left on a narrow path marked with green/white signs. Very soon the path crosses a dirt track and continues straight on its other side.

Follow the narrow path, mainly uphill, for about 10min to reach a dirt track. ▶ Ignore the green/white signed path that branches off to the right just before you reach a dirt track. Go right on the dirt track and a few minutes later arrive at a junction. Turn right and follow the stony track lined with pine trees and rock roses. There are some faint yellow arrows on trees.

As you walk uphill there are strawberry trees, lentisk and rock roses by the path.

The track climbs uphill and bends left; soon there are great views to the Mesaoria plain on your left, but then pines obstruct the views as you climb uphill on the stony track for about 15min.

The track levels out and you walk through a small clearing. A track leaves to the left towards the forest, but keep straight on as the faint yellow mark and cairns suggest. Soon the track becomes a narrow path and runs along a rocky hillside with fine views of the Kyrenia range to the west and towards Nicosia/Lefkoşa, with the Troodos mountains in the background. You might have to step over fallen trees as you progress on the rock rose-covered mountainside and then beneath pine trees.

At a junction, go left as the green/white sign suggests and soon pass some boulders as you descend the rock-scattered hillside.

Arrive at the ruins of the **Plataniotissa monastery** about 1hr 15min after leaving Alevkaya. The path curves around the site; ignore a path running downhill to the left and walk entirely around the ruins. The path then leaves the ruins to the left and runs between pines, cypresses and old carob trees.

Soon reach an old retaining wall. The path continues slightly to the left, but look for a path going uphill to the right. Follow this on the right, uphill. ▶ Ascend with

There are some faint green, red, yellow and blue paint marks on the rocks.

View from the track approaching Girne Kayasi

views to the pine-covered mountain on the right. After a rocky section, arrive at a junction. Go right and follow this path for about 15–20min: it runs close to a narrow tarmac road and then descends on steps to the road. Cross the road and arrive at **Girne Kayasi** picnic site and viewpoint. The trail continues to the right, but first you might like to admire the views towards the coast from a viewing platform.

The clear path – here signed with a green 'B' – goes downhill beneath pines. It then gradually becomes wider and about 10–15min from Girne Kayasi arrives at a dirt track. Cross it and continue on its other side by the **P78 pyramid** (T20 trail). Walk across a grassy area towards a hill and soon pass the remains of an old **mosaic** floor. The path then bends to the left.

Views to the coast accompany you as you follow the contour of the mountainside slightly downhill. About 30min after leaving Girne Kayasi, follow a steep downhill section and arrive at the ruins of the **Armenian monastery**, and a tarmac road.

SOURP MAGAR (ARMENIAN MONASTERY)

Courtyard of the Armenian monastery

This was probably founded as a Coptic monastery dedicated to Saint Macarius of Alexandria at the beginning of the 11th century. It was given to the Armenians in Cyprus at the beginning of the 15th century. The buildings were used as a resting place by pilgrims and as a school for orphans.

Since 1974 the monastery has been neglected and is now in ruins. You can wander among old fruit trees in the monastery's courtyard.

After visiting the monastery, go back to the tarmac road. Keep left on the road and a few metres later leave it to the left on a dirt track by the monastery wall as the green/white sign indicates. At the junction at the end of the wall, keep right uphill by the **P83 pyramid** (T17). ▶

Ignore the small path on the right, and after an uphill section just before reaching a tarmac road, go left. The steep, narrow path continues uphill. Ignore a faint path on the left just before the path narrows and starts steeply uphill.

On the ascent there are green, red and yellow marks.

Pass large boulders and arrive at a narrow tarmac road and **Oney Semsettin picnic site**. Go left on the road and a few metres later meet another tarmac road; keep left. About 100m later reach a small road junction; carry straight on back to the café and **Alevkaya picnic site**.

WALK 39
Alevkaya circular

Start/Finish	Alevkaya picnic site (N35.28606; E33.53278)
Distance	6km (3¾ miles)
Ascent/Descent	290m/290m
Grade	3 (due to route-finding difficulties)
Time	2hr
Refreshments	Café and water fountain at Alevkaya picnic site
Access	From Besparmak Buffavento restaurant on the Besparmak Caddesi road between Kyrenia/Girne and Nicosia/Lefkoşa, take the narrow winding tarmac road 9km to Alevkaya. The picnic site is obvious and there is space for parking.

Starting from the popular picnic site in Alevkaya, this hidden and forgotten trail, overgrown with rock roses and shrubs, offers some excellent views towards the coast and the Kyrenia mountain range. Whispering trees and birdsong accompany you on this peaceful walk. From Alevkaya there is a more popular path (Walk 38) but on this short circular walk you can include a visit to the Armenian monastery.

Red, green and white circles and green 'B' signs can be seen here.

Start from the picnic site near the herbarium at Alevkaya. Follow the tarmac road towards Buffavento and a few minutes later, at a junction, carry straight on to reach the next picnic site (**Oney Semsettin**). Keep right and just before the barrier go right and downhill on a narrow path. ◄

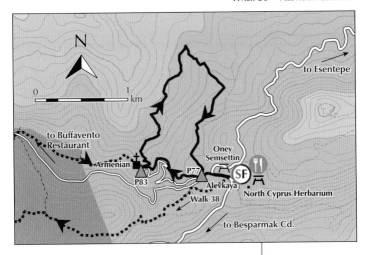

Descend on the stony path and get close to a tarmac road but turn sharply right downhill just before reaching it. Continue on the pine-lined path with a small ravine on your right. About 20min after leaving Alevkaya, arrive at the **Armenian monastery**.

> The **monastery** was once a resting place for pilgrims and a school for orphans. It was gifted to the Armenians in Cyprus in the 15th century but has been left to ruin since 1974.

Turn right by the **P83 pyramid** and the green/white marked path runs downhill; it bends left and arrives at the wall of the monastery. The path is not visible here, but go close to the building, and by the wall look for steps leading down into a very overgrown area. On these steps, look for a green sign. Go down the worn steps and cross the overgrown area diagonally towards the white rocks. (You might see a very faint path as you progress through the bushes.) Reach the white rock wall, where you will find another green sign. The path is more visible here and it continues along a ledge.

Route-finding can be difficult on the section of the trail after the monastery

The thick vegetation is mainly rock roses but there are some cypresses, a few pines and you might also see olive trees and a few carob trees near the path.

There is a ravine on your left and soon you have some views towards the coast. The path curves right. ◄ As you descend, look for green signs on the rocks. About 20min after leaving the walls of the monastery the path bends left, passes a concrete reservoir and then follows the contour of the mountainside downhill. This downhill section is dominated by dense vegetation.

You might have to step over a fallen olive tree, and soon arrive at a clearing. There is a green sign on a rock; go around an olive tree and go right downhill on a faint path. Often the path is not more than a narrow passage between rock roses. Go around boulders and continue steeply uphill. The path then levels out for a while and runs between rock roses before ascending again.

At the grassy area with cypresses on the right, turn sharply right and slightly uphill. (The path might be difficult to see here.) At a junction where two faint paths meet, go sharply right and slightly uphill among bushes. This is a faint path but you'll find red, green and blue paint marks. ▶

Arrive at a wide track and turn right. A few minutes later, in a grassy clearing, follow the green/white marks. The wide track reverts to a narrow path and continues uphill. Passing some boulders, zigzag uphill for about 10min and arrive on a dirt track. Turn right and follow this dirt track – ignoring any tracks joining from left or right – back to the **Oney Semsettin** picnic site. Go across the picnic site and on the tarmac road turn left and walk back to **Alevkaya**.

There are some pines towering above the rock roses and views open up to the Kyrenia mountain range, Besparmak Mountain and beyond.

WALK 40
Esentepe – Antiphonitis Monastery

Start/Finish	SW corner of Esentepe village (N35.33313 E33.58300)
Distance	12km (7½ miles); via alternative return: 14km (8¾ miles)
Ascent/Descent	600m/600m; via alternative return: 510m/510m
Grade	2
Time	4hr; via alternative return: 4hr (+ allow time to visit the monastery)
Refreshments	There is a small café by the monastery that is open during visiting hours.
Access	Esentepe is accessible from the New Coastal Road (D54) about 24km east of Kyrenia/Girne. There is space to park near the trail gate at the start of the walk.

From Esentepe, the route follows dirt tracks and an old forest track to Antiphonitis Monastery. The old forest track runs in the shade of trees and you can enjoy views along the way. For a small fee you can visit the monastery and admire the remains of frescos dating from the 12th century.

You can either return to Esentepe village by retracing your steps or via an alternative route following the tarmac road and a network of dirt tracks.

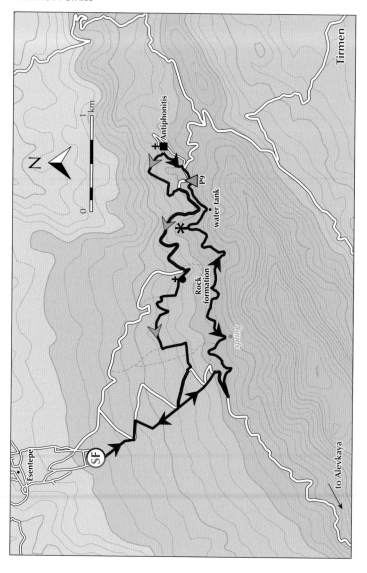

From the trail gate, walk up the dirt track towards the mountains. Soon you will see some green/white circle signs; pass a fenced area and a few minutes later reach an asphalt road. Turn right on this asphalt road and follow it slightly uphill. About 150–200m later, leave the road to the right on a dirt track and follow it towards the mountains. A few minutes later, at a junction, turn left and slightly uphill.

There is a gorge on your right and ahead the view is dominated by mountains. The track comes close to the asphalt road, but continue straight on, on the dirt track. At the next junction, keep left and slightly uphill. You soon get very close to the asphalt road again but stay on the dirt track and continue straight on.

A few minutes later, when you reach an asphalt road, turn right and follow the road for a few hundred metres with views on your right. At a junction, an old forest track leaves the asphalt road to the left. There is a sign:

Column-like rock formation seen from the forest track

'Andifonidis 4km' (Antiphonitis). You will be on this old forest track, which follows the contour of the mountain, for about an hour.

A few minutes after joining the forest track, ignore the dirt track on the right and continue straight on. ◄ Two consecutive tracks join from the left; keep right both times and arrive at a small **spring** with a picnic area.

Pines cover the slope, and views to the sea and Esentepe village accompany you.

Cross a fire break on the hillside and pass **rock formations** on your left. You might notice a faint path; ignore it. Also ignore the dirt track on the right and follow the green/white circle signs as the track traces the contour of the mountain. You will soon see the asphalt road snaking down below. Pass by a huge concrete **water tank**.

About an hour after joining the forest track, arrive at an asphalt road with a sign pointing towards the monastery. Cross the road by the **P9 pyramid** (T70 trail) and go downhill on the asphalt road as the green 'B' sign indicates. A few metres later, leave the asphalt road to the left on a path marked with a green 'B'. Zigzag downhill for about 10min and arrive at the **Antiphonitis monastery**.

ANTIPHONITIS MONASTERY

A church was built on this site – as part of a monastery – in the 12th century. The narthex and the arcade were added in the 15th century. The dome is held up by eight pillars and Antiphonitis is the only remaining example of this type of building in Cyprus. Once the interior was decorated with frescos; today you can still admire some of them.

The monastery is also known for the fact that some of the remains of the lower parts of frescos are heavily overwritten by pilgrims. You can spot dates from the 19th and 20th

The oldest frescos of Antiphonitis Monastery date from the 12th century

206

centuries carved into the wall. Some of the frescos were stolen and sold internationally after 1974; icons were found in a private collection in the Netherlands. After years of legal battles, four icons have been returned to Cyprus.

You can view the interior wall paintings for a small fee. Visiting hours: Apr–Oct, 8.30am–5pm; Nov–Mar, 8.30am–3.30pm.

After visiting the monastery you can either retrace your steps or take the alternative route back to Esentepe village.

Alternative return to Esentepe
Leave the churchyard through the gate, keep right and take a narrow path going uphill on the left. The path curves up the slope and then bends left. When it splits, go left and uphill towards an electricity pole. As you climb, the path might not be clearly visible, but head towards the electricity pole, pass it and you will see the asphalt road. Reach the tarmac road, keep right and follow this road for about 15–20min.

Ignore the dirt tracks and a fire break on the right, and then a track on the left. When you see the roof of an old church hidden by trees on the mountainside, look out for a path on the left. (It is visible just after a track joining from the left.) Follow this faint, narrow path, pass olive trees and climb up the rocky hillside. Then keep right, follow the narrow, slightly overgrown path and arrive at a small **church**.

Go around the building and continue downhill on the dirt track. Ignore the first dirt track on the left, and go downhill on the second dirt track on the left. At a junction – about 15–20min after the church – carry straight on, and a few minutes later ignore the path that joins from left, and keep straight on again. At a clearing bear left, slightly uphill.

The track bends right; at the junction keep straight on and note the green/white circle signs. Ignore the track on the right and keep straight on. At the junction go right,

A forgotten old church surrounded by old olive trees

join the tarmac road and keep right downhill. A few minutes later leave the tarmac road to the left on a dirt track slightly to the right, running parallel to the asphalt road. At the junction go right, reach a tarmac road and keep left. The dirt track leaves the asphalt road to the left; follow it back to the trail gate where you started the walk.

WALK 41

Kucuk Erenkoy circular

Start/Finish	Sinya Guest House, Kucuk Erenkoy (N35.36305 E33.67827)
Distance	6.5km (4 miles)
Ascent/Descent	300m/300m
Grade	1
Time	2hr
Refreshments	Sinya Guest House
Access	Sinya Guest House is located in Kucuk Erenkoy by the New Coastal (D54) Road. There is space to park near the guest house.

The first and last sections of this walk follow dirt tracks, however the middle section offers some fine views towards the coast as you walk along a narrow path. You will also squeeze through a narrow gap between boulders and walk through a tunnel. It is advisable to take a torch.

The trail gate is located by Sinya Guest House. Walk along the main road in the direction of Kyrenia/Girne and turn left towards the **Crystal Bay Marina** buildings. (It is the first left about 2min after the guest house.) Follow the road with the mountains in front of you and with the white modern apartments on your right. A few minutes later reach a dirt track, which starts just after the

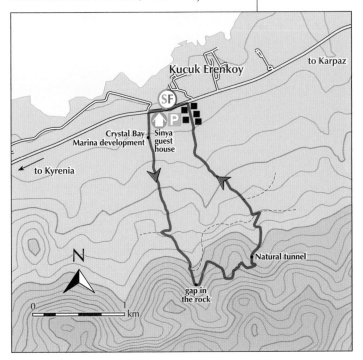

apartment blocks. Continue straight on with a ravine on your right towards the mountains. Ignore the track joining from the left and keep straight on.

At a junction, go left as the yellow arrow indicates. ◄ After a very gentle uphill section reach a clearing, and about 30min into the walk in the shade of pines a narrow path leaves the dirt track to the right (a yellow painted sign on the tree marks the path). Climb up the worn wooden steps. A few minutes later reach a rock wall with a narrow **gap**, which you will have to squeeze through.

The views in front of you and on your right are dominated by mountains.

Continue on the very narrow path with a rock towering on your right. Follow this path with some views for about 30min.

Reach a ridge where you are greeted with fine views of the village and the coast as well as of the nearby mountains. The path then leaves the ridge to the right. Zigzag steeply downhill and ignore the path joining from the left.

About 20min after leaving the ridge, walk through a gorge and arrive at the entrance of a **tunnel**. Go through the tunnel.

The return route follows a deep gorge back to the village

After emerging from the tunnel, continue through the small gorge but soon leave it as you walk uphill. Arrive

at a dirt track; turn left and slightly downhill (a yellow arrow indicates the direction). At the next junction turn right and walk with a ravine on your left. ▸

The coast, with a cluster of white buildings, stretches in front of you.

Ignore the track on your right and a few minutes later also one on the left and continue straight on. Reach houses and walk straight on between the buildings and arrive at the main road. Turn left and walk back to **Sinya Guest House**, which is only a few minutes away.

WALK 42
Tatlisu circular

Start/Finish	Tatlisu picnic site (N35.36796, E33.75758)
Distance	7km (4¼ miles)
Ascent/Descent	430m/430m
Grade	3
Time	3hr
Refreshments	In Tatlisu village but none along the way.
Access	Tatlisu village can be reached from the New Coastal Road (D54). From the village, look for green signs from the mosque and follow them to the picnic site. There are plenty of places to park at the picnic site.

The route ascends on a narrow path from which you can admire fascinating rock formations, and then you can peep out of a natural rock window near the peak. From the highest point, as far as you can see, mountains dominate the views. The second part of the trail descends on a rock rose-covered hillside with impressive views.

Tatlisu Parkaru trail gate marks the beginning of the trail at the picnic site. Descend wooden steps by the trail gate, and then when the path splits, keep left. Shortly cross a streambed and go slightly uphill. ▸

In springtime the path is lined with blooming rock roses and you may spot some small orchids.

The path runs alongside a dry streambed, and about 10min after leaving the picnic site it arrives at a slightly

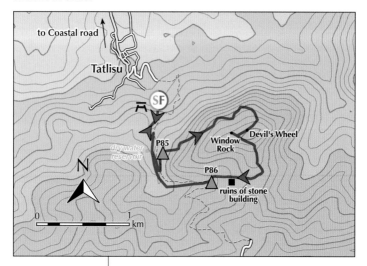

overgrown dirt track. Turn left on this track and a few minutes later reach another dirt track. Turn right and very shortly pass a **dry water reservoir**.

In the clearing, continue straight uphill as the green sign indicates and about 50m later turn sharp left on a path going steeply uphill. Arrive onto a dirt track and turn left, downhill. Approximately 150m later leave this dirt track to the right on wooden steps by the **P85 pyramid** (T36 trail).

Ascend along the rock rose-lined path with occasional glimpses of the sea and the coast on the left and with a rocky peak towering above on your right. The path is overgrown in places but there are green signs on rocks to help you to identify it. Rocky mountain peaks dominate the views on your right.

Soon arrive at a small clearing where the path is well marked and easy to follow. ◀ Continue steeply uphill with an old retaining wall on your right. The path undulates along the edge, following the contour of the mountain. Pass some interesting rock formations and about 1hr after the P85 pyramid arrive at a junction where you keep

Enjoy the views to the coast and Tatlisu village with its mosque down below on the left.

212

The highest point on the trail near Window Rock

right uphill. Ignore a path joining from the left and about 10min after the junction pass a huge semi-circular rock formation, the **Devil's Wheel**. Shortly after this, reach the rocky peak. ▸

Endless pine-covered mountains fill the horizon.

To visit the twisted tree and **Window Rock**, go straight on at the junction on the peak. A few minutes later reach the twisted tree and then arrive at the natural rock window.

Retrace your steps to the junction on the peak and continue steeply downhill as the sign indicates. The first section is on loose, very slippery gravel then the path follows the contour of the mountain with views of pine-covered hills. There is a rock wall on your left as you descend on the rock rose-covered hillside.

About 15min after leaving the peak, walk along a small ridge where you can admire the 180-degree panorama as you continue to descend along the slightly overgrown path. You might spot the rock window and the rocky peak on your right, but as you progress downhill there are pines obstructing the view. Reach a little valley with a tiny streambed on your left, and pass the **ruins** of a stone building.

About 30min after the small ridge, arrive at a dirt track with the **P86 pyramid**. The path – marked with green signs – continues on its other side, slightly to the right. Soon pass an old retaining wall and arrive at a wide track. Turn right. Where it splits, keep left and reach the point where the path goes uphill on your right. Continue straight on and retrace your steps to the **picnic site**.

WALK 43
Kantara Castle

Start/Finish	Kantara Restaurant, Kantara village (N35.38784 E33.89818)
Distance	10km (6¼ miles); return on tarmac road: 8.5km (5¼ miles)
Ascent/Descent	320m/320m; return on tarmac road: 330m/330m
Grade	1
Time	3hr; return on tarmac road: 2hr 10min (for both options allow time to visit the castle)
Refreshments	Kantara Restaurant in Kantara village
Access	From the New Coast Road (D54) take the road towards Kaplica. Leaving Kaplica village, follow the winding road for 6km to Kantara. There are plenty of places to park in front of Kantara Restaurant.

From Kantara village the undulating dirt track takes you to a castle nestled on rocks. The track curves around the rocky peak before reaching the castle's entrance, giving an opportunity to enjoy great views of the ruins from different angles.

The ruins – guarding their secrets – are perched on the rocky mountain peak, watching over the coastline, the Karpaz/Karpass and the Kyrenia mountain range. You can enjoy some marvellous views from here. The trail is signposted with green 'B' signs and is easy to follow. You can either retrace your steps or walk back to Kantara village on a tarmac road.

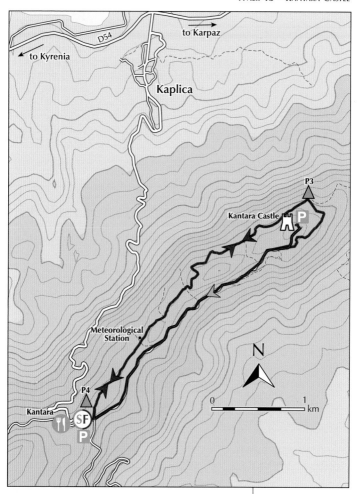

Facing the restaurant, go right and follow the green 'B' signs painted on the tarmac road. A few metres later the **P4 pyramid** and a wooden trail gate mark the beginning of the trail on the left.

Walk uphill on the stony dirt track, passing some abandoned houses. After the buildings, ignore a track on the right and continue straight uphill on the rock rose-lined dirt track. Less than 10min after the trail gate there are the first glimpses of the coast and sea on the left before the vegetation hides the views for a while.

Continue straight on the dirt track as you cross a fire break, and a few minutes later at the junction near a **meteorological station**, keep straight on downhill. There are rock formations towering on your right and views to the coast accompany you on the left as you follow the undulating track.

Ignore the track on the left and continue straight on as the green 'B' sign indicates. Soon a rocky hill with antennae and a small building on its peak appears in front of you. At the next junction keep straight uphill and a few minutes later note the track running towards the mountain with antennae – but continue as the green 'B' sign shows.

After a steep downhill section the track bends sharply to the right and runs through forest. Ignore the track on the right and continue straight on with some views to the coast on the left. About 50min after leaving Kantara village, the castle – nestled on the rocky mountain – comes into view in front of you.

The track splits in a clearing; go left and shortly spot a green 'B' sign. Kantara Castle is on your right as you pass boulders. After the boulders the track goes downhill and curves around the mountain with the castle on its peak. After a very steep downhill section arrive at a dirt track.

The **P3 pyramid** (T35) marks this junction. The green 'B' goes left, but keep right on the dirt track as the yellow and red arrows indicate. Follow this dirt track for about 20min, ignoring a track on the right. As you get closer to the castle there are excellent views towards the coast and the remains of the castle nestled on the rocks.

Arrive at a tarmac road, bear right and walk to **Kantara Castle**.

KANTARA CASTLE

Kantara Castle

The name 'Kantara' means bridge or arch in Arabic. The castle was built by the Byzantines as a lookout post as its location gave great views to both coastlines. From here smoke signals were sent to Buffavento Castle (Walk 37).

Legend has it that when the builders went to get payment for their work, the queen threw them out of her window because she didn't have enough money to pay them. Later she jumped out of the very same window. There are similar legends about the other castles.

Kantara Castle was first mentioned in AD1191, when Richard the Lionheart captured Isaac Komnenos here. The castle was then rebuilt by the Lusignans during the 12th century. The Venetians took it over and used it but by 1525 it was abandoned, as the other forts in Kyrenia/Girne, Famagusta/Gazimağusa and Nicosia/Lefkoşa became more dominant.

You can visit the castle for a small fee. Opening hours: 10am–5pm in summer; 9am–2.45pm the rest of the year.

As it is not a very long walk, you can retrace your steps to Kantara village, but if you want to get back to

Magnificent view to the east from the castle

Kantara as fast as possible after visiting the castle you can walk back on the narrow tarmac road; this will take you about 40min.

WALK 44
Kumyali circular

Start/Finish	Outside Kumyali village (N35.43480, E34.13396)
Distance	8.5km (5¼ miles)
Ascent/Descent	80m/80m
Grade	1
Time	2hr 30min
Refreshments	None
Access	The starting point is located about 500m north of Kumyali village at an intersection on the Karpaz Anayolu road. Use GPS coordinates if possible. Parking on roadside.

There are many things to look out for on this walk, including an old quarry and the remains of a rock pool. Sadly these features are not marked and there is little information about them. Meanwhile, goats graze lazily in the shade of olive trees with the sea in the background. The route follows red and white signs painted on rocks and provides some fine views.

From the information board at the start point, take the dirt track marked with a red sign and a few minutes later arrive at a small **chapel**. The trail gate is located near the chapel. Follow the red paint marks on rocks as you walk on a juniper-dotted area towards the sea. ▶

Soon arrive at a junction and go left on the well-defined rocky path. Pass an **old quarry** on your left with views to the sea on your right. About 30min from the start, descend steeply and arrive at a dirt track. Go right along this dirt track and a few minutes later, at a junction, keep left. A few metres later at the next junction go left again and follow the dirt track towards east as the red marks indicate.

Soon look out for some numbers on your left: they mark remains, but there is no information or explanation of the numbered places. A few minutes later in a road bend on your right are the remains of some **ancient arte-facts**. At a junction go left, and soon pass by a **goat pen**. There are some olive and carob trees on your left.

About 40min after joining the dirt track, pass by a **stone quarry** and a building, and shortly after that arrive at the **P92 pyramid** and a **lagoon** a little further on. Go left on the T139 trail by the pyramid, with a riverbed on your right. Soon notice an **ancient stone gutter** leading down to the riverbed.

Look out for green and yellow marks as you follow the path among bushes. A few minutes after the gutter, go left uphill. (Green and yellow signs and a wooden plant sign help to identify the spot.) Pass behind a quarry build-ing and then keep right and walk by the quarry.

Continue along a ridge with small, juniper-dot-ted rocky hills on your right. At the end of the quarry,

There is a bench beneath a carob tree as you walk with views towards the sea on your right.

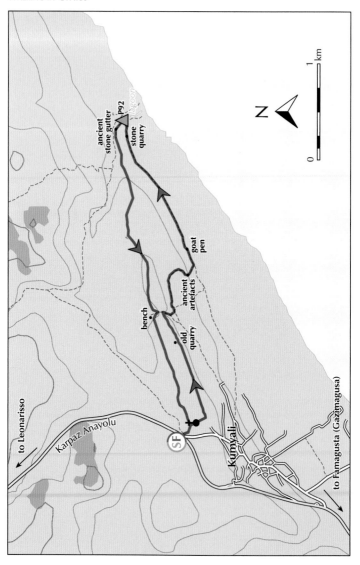

Views to the meadows hugged by low hills

continue slightly to the right, as the red and white marks indicate. Follow the red and white marks as you walk on a grassy area with junipers. Soon reach a retaining wall where there is a yellow walker sign on an olive tree.

In a big grassy area, follow the red signs on the rocks. The path runs among junipers, with some views to the sea on the left. Soon the path bends sharply to the right and goes downhill. Pass a pine tree and arrive at a dirt track. Go left, and at the junction go right, and a few metres later a narrow path starts uphill on the left.

Climb up as the green and yellow signs indicate, and then the path curves right and towards the north. Pass a **bench** and follow the red signs. Walk on a small plateau with junipers and some cypress. The path changes into a wide track and about 20min after the last bench you arrive back at the small **chapel**. Follow the dirt track back to the information board.

APPENDIX A

Route summary table

Walk	Start/Finish	Distance	Time	Grade	Ascent/Descent	Page
Southern Cyprus						
The west and the Akamas Peninsula						
1	Bath of Aphrodite	7.5km (4½ miles)	3hr	2	500m	35
2	Bath of Aphrodite	7.5km (4½ miles)	2hr 30min	1	400m	39
3A	Smigies picnic site	6.5km (4 miles)	2hr	1	180m	43
3B	Smigies picnic site	3km (1¾ miles)	1hr 15min	1	175m	47
4	Near Toxeftra Beach	11.5km (7 miles) or 10.5km (6½ miles)	4hr 30min–5hr or 6hr	3	440m or 320m	48
5	Pano Argaka	10.5km (6½ miles)	2hr 40min	1	300m	54
6	Locality Platanouthkia	5km (3 miles)	1hr 30min–2hr	1	460m	58
7	Pano Panagia	8.5km (5¼ miles) or 10.5km (6½ miles)	3hr or 3hr 40min	2	340m or 460m	61
8	Sinti Monastery	17km (10½ miles)	4hr 30min–5hr	2	290m	65
9	Kelefos Bridge	16km (10 miles) or 11km (6¾ miles)	5hr 30min or 3hr 45min	3	750m or 560m/440m	71

Walk	Start/Finish	Distance	Time	Grade	Ascent/Descent	Page
The Troodos and central Cyprus						
10	Xistarouda picnic site	12km (7½ miles)	5hr–5hr 20min	2	760m	78
11	Prodromos Dam picnic site	9.5km (6 miles)	3hr	1	420m	82
12	Near Agios Nikolaos tis Stegis church/Troodos Square	10.2km (6¾ miles)	4hr 30min	3	1050m/210m	85
13	Kampos tou Livadiou picnic site/ Agios Nikolaos tis Stegis church	13km (8 miles)	4hr	3	350m/1250m	91
14	Troodos Square	14km (8¾ miles)	4hr–4hr 30min	2	625m	95
15	Troodos Square or F953 road	12km (7½ miles) or 7km (4½ miles)	3hr 40min or 2hr 30min	2 or 1	430m or 280m	100
16	Pano Platres	9km (5½ miles)	3hr	2	570m	104
17	Pano Platres	9km (5½ miles)	3hr	2	610m	108
18	Amiantos	4km (2½ miles)	1hr 30min	1	190m	111
19	Locality Doxa Soi o Theos	13km (8 miles) or 16.5km (10¼ miles)	5hr or 6hr	3	900m or 1080m	114
20	Kannavia village	19km (11¾ miles)	5hr 30min–6hr	3	1310m	119
21	Agios Theodoros	12km (7½ miles)	4hr	1	540m	125
22	Lagoudera	15km (9¼ miles)	5hr–5hr 30min	2	1240m	129
23	Near Machairas Monastery	12km (7½ miles)	4hr	1	380m	133

Walk	Start/Finish	Distance	Time	Grade	Ascent/Descent	Page
24	Machairas Monastery or Kionia picnic site/Fikardou	5km (3 miles) or 10km (6¼ miles)	2hr or 3hr 45min	2	310m/280m or 600m/980m	136
25	Paylias-Dhyo Mouttes trail head or Kionia picnic site	20km (12½ miles)	6hr	3	1300m	141
26	Near Kionia picnic site	12km (7½ miles)	4hr	3	670m	146
South and east						
27	Kato Archimandrita	10km (6¼ miles)	3hr	1	430m	150
28	Pissouri Beach	11km (6¾ miles)	4hr	3	640m	153
29	Germasogeia Dam	12km (7½ miles)	4hr	2	750m	157
30	Cape Greco	6km (3¾ miles)	2hr	1	165m	160
31	Cape Greco	6.6km (4 miles)	2hr	1	165m	163
Northern Cyprus						
32	Near Kalkanli	8km (5 miles)	2hr 40min	1	90m	169
33	Karsiyaka village	5km (3 miles)	1hr 45min	1	290m	172
34	Lapta	12km (7½ miles)	5hr 30min	3	830m	175
35	Agirdag	9.5km (6 miles)	3hr 30min	2	500m	180
36	Zeytinlik village	11.5km (7 miles)	5hr	3	760m	183
37	Besparmak	18.5km (11½ miles)	7hr	3	1150m	188
38	Alevkaya	9km (5½ miles)	3hr 30min–4hr	2	430m	195

Walk	Start/Finish	Distance	Time	Grade	Ascent/Descent	Page
39	Alevkaya	6km (3¾ miles)	2hr	3	290m	200
40	Esentepe	12km (7½ miles) or 14km (8¾ miles)	4hr	2	600m or 510m	203
41	Kucuk Erenkoy	6.5km (4 miles)	2hr	1	300m	208
42	Tatlisu	7km (4¼ miles)	3hr	3	430m	211
43	Kantara village	10km (6¼ miles) or 8.5km (5¼ miles)	3hr or 2hr 10min	1	320m or 330m	214
44	Near Kumyali village	8.5km (5¼ miles)	2hr 30min	1	80m	218

APPENDIX B
Useful contacts

Tourist information
Cyprus Tourism Organisation
www.visitcyprus.com

Official site of Troodos mountains
www.mytroodos.com

Troodos Visitor Centre
tel +357 2542 0144

Paphos/Baf information
www.visitpafos.org.cy

Tourist information offices

Southern Cyprus
Nicosia/Lefkoşa
tel +357 2267 4264

Limassol
tel +357 2532 3211

Platres
tel +357 2542 1316

Larnaca
tel +357 2465 4322

Paphos/Baf
tel +357 2693 2841

Agia Napa
tel +357 2372 1796

Polis
tel +357 2632 2468

Northern Cyprus
Nicosia/Lefkosa
tel +90 392 227 2994

Kyrenia/Girne (Harbour)
tel +90 392 815 6079

Famagusta/Gazimagusa
tel +90 392 366 2864

Ercan Airport
tel +90 392 231 4003

Transport

Airports
Larnaca International Airport
www.hermesairports.com
tel +357 2400 8368

Paphos International Airport
www.hermesairports.com
tel +357 2600 7368

Flight operators (from UK)
Easyjet
www.easyjet.com

Ryanair
www.ryanair.com

British Airways
www.britishairways.com

Jet2
www.jet2.com

Thomas Cook
www.thomascook.com

Local bus operators
Intercity Buses
www.intercity-buses.com

Pafos Buses
www.pafosbuses.com

Cyprus By Bus
www.cyprusbybus.com

Limassol Airport Express
www.limassolairportexpress.eu

Limassol Buses
www.limassolbuses.com

Car rental

Southern Cyprus
In Southern Cyprus you will find the well-known international car rental companies such as Europcar, Sixt, Avis, Hertz, Budget, Alamo and Enterprise, as well as local car hire companies such as Drive Cyprus. Details can be found online using an internet search engine.

Northern Cyprus
The British Rent-a-Car
www.britishrentacar.com
tel +90 533 851 73 48

Sun Rent-a-Car
www.sunrentacar.com
tel + 90 392 227 23 03

Pacific Rentals
www.pacific-rentals.com
tel +90 542 852 1920

Kyrenia Castle Rent-a-Car
www.kyreniacastle.com
tel +90 533 841 80 01

Ferries
www.ferries-turkey.com

www.akgunlerbilet.com

Accommodation
Cyprus listings
www.cyprus.com

Bookcyprus.com
www.bookcyprus.com

Booking.com
www.booking.com

Trivago
www.trivago.co.uk

Expedia
www.expedia.co.uk

APPENDIX C
Further reading

Books

Lawrence Durrell, *Bitter Lemons of Cyprus*, Faber & Faber, 1951

Victoria Hislop, *The Sunrise*, Headline Review, 2015

Stella Kalogeraki, *Greek Mythology*, Mediterraneo Editions, 2004

Gregory S Lamb, *The People In Between: Cyprus Odyssey*, CreateSpace, 2012

John McPhee, *Annals of the Former World*, Farrar, Straus and Giroux, 1998

George Sfikas, *Wild Flowers of Cyprus*, Efstathiadis Group, 1992

Websites

www.greekmythology.com (Greek mythology)

www.ancient.eu/cyprus (ancient history)

www.cypruswildflowers.com (nature)

www.aboutcyprus.org.cy (history, nature, culture)

DOWNLOAD THE ROUTE IN GPX FORMAT

All the routes in this guide are available for download from:

www.cicerone.co.uk/837/GPX

as GPX files. You should be able to load them into most formats of mobile device, whether GPS or smartphone.

When you go to this link, you will be asked for your email address and where you purchased the guide, and have the option to subscribe to the Cicerone e-newsletter.

www.cicerone.co.uk

LISTING OF CICERONE GUIDES

The Danube Cycleway Volume 1
The Rhine Cycle Route
The Westweg
Walking in the Bavarian Alps

ICELAND AND GREENLAND
Trekking in Greenland
Walking and Trekking in Iceland

IRELAND
The Irish Coast to Coast Walk
The Mountains of Ireland

ITALY
Italy's Sibillini National Park
Shorter Walks in the Dolomites
Ski Touring and Snowshoeing in
the Dolomites
The Way of St Francis
Through the Italian Alps
Trekking in the Apennines
Trekking in the Dolomites
Via Ferratas of the Italian
Dolomites: Vol 1
Via Ferratas of the Italian
Dolomites: Vol 2
Walking in Abruzzo
Walking in Italy's Stelvio
National Park
Walking in Sardinia
Walking in Sicily
Walking in the Dolomites
Walking in Umbria
Walking on the Amalfi Coast
Walking the Italian Lakes
Walks and Treks in the
Maritime Alps

SCANDINAVIA
Walking in Norway

EASTERN EUROPE
AND THE BALKANS
The Danube Cycleway Volume 2
The High Tatras
The Mountains of Romania
Walking in Bulgaria's
National Parks
Walking in Hungary
Mountain Biking in Slovenia
The Islands of Croatia
The Julian Alps of Slovenia
The Mountains of Montenegro
Trekking in Slovenia
Walking in Croatia
Walking in Slovenia:
The Karavanke

SPAIN
Coastal Walks in Andalucia

Cycle Touring in Spain
Mountain Walking in
Southern Catalunya
Spain's Sendero Histórico:
The GR1
The Mountains of Nerja
The Northern Caminos
The Sierras of Extremadura
The Way of St James
Cyclist Guide
Trekking in Mallorca
Walking in Andalucia
Walking in Mallorca
Walking in Menorca
Walking in the
Cordillera Cantabrica
Walking in the Sierra Nevada
Walking on Gran Canaria
Walking on La Gomera and
El Hierro
Walking on La Palma
Walking on Lanzarote
and Fuerteventura
Walking on Tenerife
Walking on the Costa Blanca
Walking the GR7 in Andalucia
Walks and Climbs in the
Picos de Europa

PORTUGAL
Walking in Madeira
Walking in the Algarve

GREECE
The High Mountains of Crete
Walking and Trekking on Corfu

CYPRUS
Walking in Cyprus

MALTA
Walking on Malta

INTERNATIONAL CHALLENGES,
COLLECTIONS AND ACTIVITIES
Canyoning in the Alps
The Via Francigena
Canterbury to Rome – Part 2

AFRICA
Climbing in the Moroccan
Anti-Atlas
Kilimanjaro:
A Complete Trekker's Guide
Mountaineering in the Moroccan
High Atlas
The High Atlas
Trekking in the Atlas Mountains
Walking in the Drakensberg

ASIA
Jordan – Walks, Treks, Caves,
Climbs and Canyons
Treks and Climbs in Wadi Rum,
Jordan
Annapurna
Everest: A Trekker's Guide
Trekking in the Himalaya
Bhutan
Trekking in Ladakh
The Mount Kailash Trek

NORTH AMERICA
British Columbia
The Grand Canyon
The John Muir Trail
The Pacific Crest Trail

SOUTH AMERICA
Aconcagua and the
Southern Andes
Hiking and Biking Peru's
Inca Trails
Torres del Paine

TECHNIQUES
Geocaching in the UK
Indoor Climbing
Lightweight Camping
Map and Compass
Outdoor Photography
Polar Exploration
Rock Climbing
Sport Climbing
The Hillwalker's Manual

MINI GUIDES
Alpine Flowers
Avalanche!
Navigation
Pocket First Aid and
Wilderness Medicine
Snow

MOUNTAIN LITERATURE
8000 metres
A Walk in the Clouds
Abode of the Gods
The Pennine Way – the Path,
the People, the Journey
Unjustifiable Risk?

For full information on all our
guides, books and eBooks,
visit our website:
www.cicerone.co.uk

Walking – Trekking – Mountaineering – Climbing – Cycling

Over 40 years, Cicerone have built up an outstanding collection of over 300 guides, inspiring all sorts of amazing adventures.

Every guide comes from extensive exploration and research by our expert authors, all with a passion for their subjects. They are frequently praised, endorsed and used by clubs, instructors and outdoor organisations.

All our titles can now be bought as **e-books**, **ePubs** and **Kindle** files and we also have an online magazine – **Cicerone Extra** – with features to help cyclists, climbers, walkers and trekkers choose their next adventure, at home or abroad.

Our website shows any **new information** we've had in since a book was published. Please do let us know if you find anything has changed, so that we can publish the latest details. On our **website** you'll also find great ideas and lots of detailed information about what's inside every guide and you can buy **individual routes** from many of them online.

It's easy to keep in touch with what's going on at Cicerone by getting our monthly **free e-newsletter**, which is full of offers, competitions, up-to-date information and topical articles. You can subscribe on our home page and also follow us on **Facebook** and **Twitter** or dip into our **blog**.

Cicerone – the very best guides for exploring the world.

CICERONE

Juniper House, Murley Moss, Oxenholme Road, Kendal, Cumbria LA9 7RL
Tel: 015395 62069 info@cicerone.co.uk
www.cicerone.co.uk and **www.cicerone-extra.com**